# Creating
# Literacy-Rich
## Schools for
# Adolescents

Gay Ivey

Douglas Fisher

ASCD

Alexandria, Virginia USA

1703 N. Beauregard St. • Alexandria, VA 22311-1714 USA
Phone: 800-933-2723 or 703-578-9600 • Fax: 703-575-5400
Web site: www.ascd.org • E-mail: member@ascd.org
Author guidelines: www.ascd.org/write

Gene R. Carter, *Executive Director;* Nancy Modrak, *Director of Publishing;* Julie Houtz, *Director of Book Editing & Production;* Leah Lakins, *Project Manager;* Greer Beeken, *Graphic Designer;* Circle Graphics, *Typesetter;* Vivian Coss, *Production Specialist*

All Web links in this book are correct as of the publication date below but may have become inactive or otherwise modified since that time. If you notice a deactivated or changed link, please e-mail books@ascd.org with the words "Link Update" in the subject line. In your message, please specify the Web link, the book title, and the page number on which the link appears.

PAPERBACK ISBN-13: 978-1-4166-0321-4     ASCD product #105142     s3/06
PAPERBACK ISBN-10: 1-4166-0321-2

*e-books editions:* retail PDF ISBN-13: 978-1-4166-0386-3; retail ISBN-10: 1-4166-0386-7
netLibrary ISBN-13: 978-1-4166-0384-9; netLibrary ISBN-10: 1-4166-0384-0
ebrary ISBN-13: 978-1-4166-0385-6; ebrary ISBN-10: 1-4166-0385-9

Also available as an e-book through ebrary, netLibrary, and many online booksellers (see Books in Print for the ISBNs).

Quantity discounts for this book: 10–49 copies, 10%; 50+ copies, 15%; for 500 or more copies, call 800-933-2723, ext. 5634, or 703-575-5634.

**Library of Congress Cataloging-in-Publication Data**

Ivey, Gay.
  Creating literacy-rich schools for adolescents / Gay Ivey and Douglas Fisher.
    p. cm.
  Includes bibliographical references and index.
  ISBN-13: 978-1-4166-0321-4 (alk. paper)
  ISBN-10: 1-4166-0321-2 (alk. paper)
1. Reading (Secondary)   I. Fisher, Douglas, 1965–   II. Title.

LB1632.I84 2006
428.4071'2–dc22

                                                    2005031957

12 11 10 09                    12 11 10 9 8 7 6 5 4 3

# Creating Literacy-Rich Schools for Adolescents

# Foreword

## by Donna Ogle

There is no more appropriate time for this pertinent and useful book to be published. Literacy levels of middle and high school students in the United States have not improved over the past 20 years, according to the 2004 National Assessment of Educational Progress. Schools are being held accountable for students' growth and are now obligated to look at the literacy development of all their students. Even as this focus has created discomfort, it has opened a window of opportunity to address literacy more deeply.

The good news is that excellent schools are stepping up to the challenge. In *Creating Literacy-Rich Schools for Adolescents*, Gay Ivey and Douglas Fisher introduce us to schools where teachers and administrators have developed a common approach to literacy focused around a small set of transportable and transparent strategies. They know how difficult it is to get teachers to add more to their priorities and they provide evidence that a whole-school effort has a much greater impact than the efforts of individual teachers. By sharing a clearly defined set of key strategies, teachers across all content areas can be part of the literacy effort. This book is filled with concrete examples that illustrate how a shared approach to literacy learning can become a central part of teaching strategies.

As literacy becomes more multifaceted and intellectually demanding for secondary school students, *Creating Literacy-Rich Schools for Adolescents* will help schools rethink their commitment to literacy. Schools now have the charge of teaching students to effectively use visual and electronic literacy.

In order to meet these new demands, all teachers need be involved in building students' knowledge and understanding of challenging content. For schools that are serious about helping students become "masters" at learning, this book will guide schools toward providing consistent opportunities for students to gain control over their learning strategies.

*Creating Literacy-Rich Schools for Adolescents* is an ideal text to use as a starting point for middle and secondary teachers to analyze their instruction and prioritize their modeling and teaching strategies. I can easily envision teachers discussing these chapters and creating action plans that deepen their commitment to literacy.

As I read the book, I kept marking places where the authors address questions I hear frequently from teachers, such questions as, "Isn't this the responsibility of the English department?" "I don't have time to teach students to read." "What can I do?" "How can we check the reading level of materials?" and "My SSR time is a waste. How can I make it worthwhile?" Teachers reading this book will find clear answers to these and many other important questions.

Ivey and Fisher also emphasize listening to students and actively involving them as learners. They show that as teachers listen more closely to students, find their strengths and weaknesses, and build resource materials that they can read, their students' literacy skills will increase.

This book is also an excellent guide for content area teachers, reading specialists, literacy coaches, librarians, special education teachers, and second language teachers. We know that the content teachers are the ones who can best model and regularly support students' strategic reading and content learning. Yet they often don't feel competent about how to guide students' engagement with content materials. Ivey and Fisher show how these educators can be a part of an all-school commitment to making literacy essential.

*Creating Literacy-Rich Schools for Adolescents* is an important resource for middle and secondary schools interested in supporting their students with the quality instruction they deserve. Thanks to Gay Ivey and Doug Fisher for sharing their experiences and providing such useful guidance to all schools that are addressing key issues in literacy and learning.

# Overture

To guide you as you read—but more important, to guide you as you examine and develop the literacy program in your own school or classroom—we have developed a set of Quality Indicators for Secondary Literacy. Each area in the table of indicators is connected to a chapter in the book and is guided by an essential question, followed by a series of indicators. To the right of each indicator, we list a continuum of possibilities for meeting each indicator, with 5 describing the most desirable practice and 1 describing the least compatible practice. As you read each chapter, you will note that we revisit the essential questions and quality indicators and provide related research-based findings and more explicit practical examples. The indicators begin on the next page.

# QUALITY INDICATORS FOR SECONDARY LITERACY (QISL)

## AREA 1: ENGLISH LANGUAGE ARTS CLASS

*1. Are students' reading and writing development and relevant life experiences used to explore literary concepts?*

| | 5 | 4 | 3 | 2 | 1 |
|---|---|---|---|---|---|
| 1.1. Universal themes are the focus, as opposed to individual texts. | Multiple texts are used that allow students to explore big ideas such as life and death, what it means to be human, or survival. | | One or two class texts are used and are based on an overall theme or question. | | One whole-class novel is used. |
| 1.2. Selected texts span a range of difficulty levels. | Multiple texts are used, and students select texts based on their interests and reading levels. | | An alternative is identified for struggling readers, or book clubs require forced choices. | | Grade-level texts are used. |
| 1.3. Reading and writing instruction and materials address contemporary and engaging issues. | Current adolescent literature and informational texts, including electronic formats, are featured prominently. Writing is used for multiple purposes, and students write across genres. | | Classics are supplemented with contemporary readings, writing is used as a way for students to communicate, and students write for multiple purposes. | | Only classics are read, and writing is limited to traditional forms such as the five-paragraph essay. |
| 1.4. Instruction builds students' reading and writing competence. | A gradual release of responsibility guides the teachers' instruction and results in increased achievement. | | Groups of students work on skill assignments that are related to the theme. | | Skill work is assigned and may appear remedial in nature. |
| 1.5. Literary devices are taught with texts that are readable and meaningful to students. | Literary devices are studied across texts and genres before students experiment with these devices in their writing. | | Literary devices are taught out of context or with texts that are too difficult for students to understand; students are not expected to write using these devices. | | Literary devices are taught as vocabulary terms to be memorized. |

## AREA 2: CONTENT AREA CLASSES
*2. Do all courses throughout a student's day capitalize on the student's literacy and language as a way to learn new information?*

| | 5 | 4 | 3 | 2 | 1 |
|---|---|---|---|---|---|
| 2.1. Big ideas are the focus of students' reading and writing. | Students construct knowledge by connecting new knowledge with prior knowledge and relevant life experiences in all of their reading and writing. | | Students read about big ideas, or themes are presented; yet assessments focus on discrete knowledge and facts. | | Reading and writing focus on discrete knowledge and skills; students are expected to memorize facts. |
| 2.2. Students are expected to read and write in every class. | Reading, writing, speaking, and listening are used throughout the period, and students have the opportunity to demonstrate their content understanding in multiple ways. | | Students read or write periodically and may be asked to demonstrate their understanding through language. | | Class instruction is lecture and recall or activity oriented; textbook reading is assigned for homework. |
| 2.3. Students are taught strategies for reading and writing increasingly complex text. | Strategy instruction is recursive to the point of becoming transparent; students use reading comprehension and writing strategies throughout the school day and year. | | Reading and writing strategies are presented to students, and students are expected to use them on their own. | | No support is provided for reading, and students are expected to respond to end-of-chapter questions. |
| 2.4. Selected texts span a range of difficulty levels. | Students learn important concepts through reading a range of texts, including informational sources, short stories, biographies, poems, diaries, journals, primary sources, graphic novels, picture books, songs, and electronic sources. | | Textbooks are supplemented with whole-class readings such as a newspaper or magazine article. | | Grade-level textbooks are used. |

## AREA 3: SUSTAINED SILENT READING/INDEPENDENT READING
*3. Are all students provided with an opportunity to read for learning and pleasure during the school day?*

| | 5 | 4 | 3 | 2 | 1 |
|---|---|---|---|---|---|
| **3.1. Instructional time is dedicated to self-selected reading.** | Daily instructional time is dedicated to self-selected reading, and school policies and procedures support the use of this time. | | Self-selected reading time is implemented inconsistently or only in selected English classes. | | Students are not provided with an opportunity to read during the school day. |
| **3.2. Students have access to diverse texts.** | School and classroom libraries are well stocked with diverse adolescent literature and informational texts; teachers actively seek out books for individual students. | | Teachers' classroom libraries are available but stagnate throughout the year, or students are expected to visit the school library to access books. | | Students read from assigned class readings or are expected to bring their own reading material. |
| **3.3. Teachers ensure that self-selected reading time matters for students.** | Teachers model reading and support students in their self-selected reading by helping them select appropriate texts, helping them get started reading, and helping them overcome dilemmas in their reading. | | Teachers model reading during self-selected reading time. | | Teachers complete other duties or lecture during self-selected reading times. |

## AREA 4: INTERVENTION AND SUPPORT FOR STRUGGLING READERS
*4. Do the intervention initiatives cause students to read more and to read better?*

| | 5 | 4 | 3 | 2 | 1 |
|---|---|---|---|---|---|
| 4.1. Teachers are actively involved in providing intervention and support. | Teachers have significant involvement in the design and delivery of the intervention. | | Teachers have some oversight, but the majority of the program is delivered by volunteers or paraprofessionals. | | Teachers have limited or no involvement; intervention is delivered in the absence of a teacher (e.g., via computer-only programs or take-home workbooks). |
| 4.2. Intervention reflects a comprehensive approach to reading and writing. | Intervention is comprehensive and integrated such that students experience reading and writing as a cohesive whole. | | Intervention includes important components of the reading processes but addresses them separately (e.g., 15 minutes of word study followed by an unrelated comprehension activity); either reading or writing is addressed, but not both. | | Intervention focuses on an isolated skill (e.g., topic sentence) or singular aspect of literacy development (e.g., phonics, phonemic awareness, fluency, vocabulary, comprehension). |
| 4.3. Intervention reading and writing is engaging. | Authentic children's and adolescent literature (fiction and nonfiction) is at the core of the intervention. | | Intervention relies on isolated paragraphs on topics selected by the intervention program. | | Program uses artificial text, no connected text-skills work. |
| 4.4. Intervention instruction is driven by useful and relevant assessments. | Teacher-administered assessments are ongoing and are used to tailor individual instruction; writing samples and text-based discussions are one type of assessment used. | | Uniform assessments are used for placement, program entry, and program exit. | | All students start at the same point and move through the intervention components regardless of their individual performance. |
| 4.5. Intervention includes significant opportunities for authentic reading and writing. | The majority of intervention time is devoted to authentic reading and writing. | | Periodic opportunities are provided for students to read or write. | | No connected reading and writing is provided or required (e.g., sole focus is on word-level activities or skills worksheets). |

## AREA 5: LEADERSHIP AND SCHOOLWIDE SUPPORT
*5. Is there a schoolwide emphasis on literacy, and does this focus develop teacher expertise?*

| | 5 | 4 | 3 | 2 | 1 |
|---|---|---|---|---|---|
| 5.1. All teachers have access to materials for reading and writing. | Funds are regularly expended on books across content areas, developmental reading levels, and students' personal reading preferences, and on technological resources. | | Limited funds are allocated for departments, classroom teachers, or the school library for purchase of books; technology is generally available in classrooms. | | No funds are available for purchase of books; computers are available in a lab. |
| 5.2. Human resources are dedicated to the schoolwide literacy plan. | Reading specialists serve as literacy instructional leaders across the curriculum; there is a schoolwide literacy council that meets regularly to establish policies and procedures related to literacy. | | Reading resource teachers or a reading specialist works with a limited number of students in pullout programs; the literacy council has no authority and meets infrequently. | | There are no certified reading specialists, and there is no literacy council supported by the administration. |
| 5.3. Professional development builds teacher knowledge and expertise. | Professional development opportunities are differentiated and job embedded, focus on increasing knowledge about literacy processes and development, and respect the teacher as a professional. | | Professional development opportunities focus on literacy but are mandated and common for all teachers. | | Professional development centers on learning about programs or textbooks. |
| 5.4. The school has a culture of collaboration and peer coaching. | Teachers are provided with opportunities to observe and give feedback to one another; teachers are regularly observed sharing ideas and books with one another. | | The school has a peer coach who provides feedback to teachers about their lessons. Teachers meet as departments to plan lessons and discuss their successes. | | Teachers operate as independent contractors and have no opportunities to observe their colleagues. There are no conversations about learning and teaching across classrooms. |
| 5.5. There is a schoolwide commitment to providing literacy assessments for the purpose of designing instruction and assessing student progress. | There is a system for creating common assessments, and all teachers review individual student performance data with their colleagues on a regular basis. These assessment conversations occur throughout the school year. | | Multiple assessments are used to determine student progress and needs; teachers volunteer to meet with one another to review student work. | | The assessments used in the school are limited to the state-mandated tests; teachers do not review assessment or test data with their peers. |

# Introduction: Adolescent Literacy in Perspective

What does it mean to be literate? More important, what does it mean to be literate in the 21st century? People answer these questions in so many different ways. For some, literacy is the ability to decode words on a page. For others, literacy is about reading and writing grade-level texts. For still others, literacy involves reading, writing, speaking, and listening—known collectively as the language arts.

Over time, the definition of what it means to be literate has changed and evolved. Conceptions of adolescent literacy in particular now consider the vital nature of the nonschool types of literacy skills and habits evident in students' out-of-school activities (such as video games and popular music), as well as the interplay of students and contexts for learning (Moje, Young, Readence, & Moore, 2000). Learning to read and reading to learn are no longer seen solely as traditional academic processes. To fully prepare students for life now and in the future, educators need to ask different questions: What will students need to know to participate more fully in a technological world? To act as productive citizens? To become critical consumers of information? To live high-quality personal lives?

Given that you are reading this, we can infer that you are interested in the literacy learning of secondary school students. We imagine that the various readers of this book come with a range of notions about what it means to be literate, but what we all likely have in common is the belief that we could be doing a better job of supporting and motivating students to use reading, writing, listening, and speaking as a way to learn and think both now and in the future. We begin with a familiar question in discussions of secondary literacy: Is every teacher a teacher of reading?

How many times have you or the teachers you work with heard the popular catchphrase that says, "Every teacher is a teacher of reading"? It has become cliché, like so many other popular education slogans, including "All children can learn." It is important to note that in each of these clichés resides a glimmer of hope, a vision of what education could be. Each of these clichés also discounts the complexities of the educational enterprise and the hard work that must be done to realize dreams.

So is every teacher a teacher of reading? Consider the following real-life scenario. A group of math teachers is sitting in a room poring over textbooks. They are an elected adoption committee from a school site who will recommend one book for their school. These teachers, and their colleagues across the content areas, have arguably had more training on "content literacy strategies" than most high school faculties (see Fisher, 2001b). A consultant comes into the room to discuss one of the textbook series. She starts by saying, "All teachers are teachers of reading, and our program helps you . . ." All the math teachers in the room cross their arms and listen politely as the consultant continues. It is clear to anyone who knows them that they will not be purchasing this series.

Following the meeting with the consultant, the group is asked about their reaction to the comment that all teachers are teachers of reading. One of them replies by asking, "Would we say that all teachers are teachers of algebraic thinking?" Another says, "It just makes me mad that our discipline seems less important and that reading is all that matters." The department chair says, "What about writing? Or speaking, for that matter? Do we not need to worry about that—just reading?"

In response, they are asked to consider their classrooms and the learning they hope to facilitate. They are asked if they think that learning requires language. As a group, they respond affirmatively. Then they are asked if "all learning is language based." Again they respond positively.

Learning requires reading, writing, speaking, listening, and viewing. Until we can download information directly into our brains (hopefully while we're sleeping), we will learn with and through literacy processes.

Thus we do not subscribe to the idea that all teachers are teachers of reading. Rather, we know that learning is language based and that all teachers have a role to play in students' understanding and use of reading, writing, speaking, listening, and viewing.

In this book, we hope not to perpetuate the "every teacher is a teacher of reading" mantra. We have seen advertisements for countless workshops and have read numerous professional materials in which middle and high school teachers are urged to "incorporate reading and writing strategies" or "teach reading within the subject areas." No doubt, the popularity of these phrases stems from the underlying belief that in order to raise students' literacy achievement, all teachers need to pitch in, and students need lots of reading *instruction*. We are completely in favor of increasing students' literacy achievement. But we would argue that, primarily, students need lots of rich, literacy-based learning *experiences* across the school day, and sometimes those experiences require specific instruction in reading, but *all have the ultimate goal of learning and thinking.*

An example from a middle school classroom will help to clarify this distinction. At the onset of a unit on the civil rights movement, a 7th grade teacher reads aloud to her class the following excerpt:

> The body had swollen to almost twice its normal size; the head had been severely beaten, "torture, horrible beating," said one deputy. One side of the victim's forehead was crushed, an eye had been ripped raw by the barbed wire wrapped around it. The beatings and three days in the river had turned the face and head into a monstrous mess of stinking flesh. The remains were so grotesque and mangled that deputies could only determine that it was a young Black male. (Crowe, 2003, p. 64)

Students were surprised to learn that the body described here refers to a 14-year-old boy, and it's just enough to make them want more information. The teacher briefly tells the story of Emmett Till and how his murder by white men, followed by the publication of a photograph of his mutilated corpse in *Jet* magazine, served as a catalyst for what would become the civil rights movement. She shows the book she has just read from, *Getting Away with Murder: The True Story of the Emmett Till Case* (Crowe, 2003), and tells students it will be available for them to read throughout the unit. Immediately, five students raise their hands to ask if they can borrow it first. Throughout the next several days, she builds students' curiosity and interest in the topic by reading excerpts from other related texts (i.e. *My Dream of*

*Martin Luther King*, Ringgold, 1995; *Now Is Your Time!*, Myers, 1991; *I've Seen the Promised Land*, Myers, 2004).

She gets students to think about the issue of civil rights, what they already know, and what they want to know by having them view a photograph appearing in Toni Morrison's picture book, *Remember: The Journey to School Integration* (2004). In this picture taken in Cambridge, Maryland, in 1963, a white restaurant owner is shown breaking raw eggs over the heads of white and black protesters kneeling on the sidewalk in front of the restaurant. The teacher asks students to write for five minutes about any images they observe in this photo, feelings it evokes, and links to their own knowledge on the topic and personal experiences.

As students progress through the study of civil rights, the teacher maintains a good balance between specific information required by the official curriculum and other high-interest angles on the topic that students find intriguing. For instance, to explore specific required topics such as bus boycotts, school segregation, and the influence of Martin Luther King, the teacher creates readers theater scripts from these three texts: *I Am Rosa Parks* (Parks, 1997), *Through My Eyes* (Bridges, 1999), and *I Have a Dream* (King, 1997). Students are divided into three groups, each taking one of the scripts to study, rehearse, and perform (see Worthy, Broaddus, & Ivey, 2001). Through repeated practice and familiarity with the text, each group is able to perform a text—that is, to read dramatically, with fluency and understanding. The gist of each topic is clear to the rest of the class as the students listen intently to their classmates, who now sound like expert readers.

Also along the way, the teacher asks students to select a topic within the overall unit that they find personally interesting and wish to study more explicitly and deeply. Students focus on a range of topics, from the life and rhetoric of Malcolm X to the Negro baseball leagues. As students read to learn and collect information from multiple sources in preparation for creating an original piece of writing on their topic, their teacher takes advantage of an opportunity to teach reading strategies that seem particularly useful to students at this point, such as how to summarize what they read and how to identify the main idea. She explores with students various genres and forms of writing, such as persuasive essays, journal entries, and newspaper articles, that might be outlets for their own work. One student, inspired by the interviews published in *Oh Freedom! Kids Talk About the Civil*

*Rights Movement with the People Who Made It Happen* (King & Osborne, 1997), sets out to do some fieldwork by interviewing members of her own family who were affected by the civil rights movement.

This brief description of a social studies classroom driven by rich, literacy-based learning experiences is a far cry from what we believe most people think of when they hear the phrase "every teacher is a teacher of reading." Reading and writing are not simply added to the curriculum. Reading instruction is not just "included." Rather, learning depends on and is enriched by engaged reading, writing, listening, and viewing. Literacy and language are fundamental to learning.

This scenario and this book are grounded in some common beliefs about literacy learning for adolescents. Recently, the people who think a lot about adolescent literacy have felt it was worthwhile to describe some principles to guide us in our thinking. In 1999 the International Reading Association published a position statement framed by a list of seven areas of support all adolescent literacy learners deserve:

• Access to a wide variety of reading material that appeals to their interests.

• Instruction that builds the skill and desire to read increasingly complex materials.

• Assessment that shows their strengths as well as their needs.

• Expert teachers who model and provide explicit instruction across the curriculum.

• Reading specialists who assist students having difficulty learning how to read.

• Teachers who understand the complexities of individual adolescent readers.

• Homes and communities that support the needs of adolescent learners.

In 2004 the National Council of Teachers of English created an additional list of guidelines for supporting adolescent learners, summarized here:

**Adolescent readers need—**

• Experiences with diverse texts and multiple perspectives.

• Authentic, student-initiated discussions about text.

- Experiences to reflect critically on their own literacy processes.
- Experiences examining texts critically.

**Teachers of adolescents need—**

- Adequate reading materials that span difficulty levels and relate to students' interests.
- Professional development that helps them to link students' personal literacy with school literacy, to use literacy within their disciplines as a way of teaching their disciplines, to identify students' dilemmas in reading and respond with appropriate support, to support student-led discussions about text, and to create contexts in which students can critically examine texts.

We have included both documents as appendices to this book, and we urge you to look at the research bases for these important recommendations.

You will notice strong connections between these suggestions and the way we describe high-quality reading instruction across the day in secondary schools in this book. Chapter 1 focuses on the all-important English classroom. Although we know that literacy as a way of learning should be evident across the school day, we know the English or language arts classroom experience is crucial for students' literacy development. We also believe that English classrooms of old times, centered on traditional instruction and classic literature, will not suit the needs of many of our students. We urge you to reexamine reading materials, writing experiences, and expectations for what students learn. In Chapter 2 we move to the content area classroom, with a focus on some solid, reliable strategies for reading and writing as well as alternatives to the one-size-fits-all textbook. Chapter 3 emphasizes the role of independent reading within the school day, and we look at not only schoolwide, sustained, self-selected reading, but also the role that independent reading can play in content learning. We tackle the often contentious but always popular topic of literacy intervention in Chapter 4. We want to give you some ways to be critical consumers of commercial programs and to design interventions with components that really matter for students still struggling to read and write. Finally, in Chapter 5 we examine the schoolwide structures that should be in place to ensure that teachers and students are supported in their pursuits of high levels of literacy and thinking. To that end, we discuss professional development, peer coaching, leadership, and assessment systems.

# 1

# Reading and Writing in English Classes

One of the many features of middle and high schools, and one that has significant instructional implications, is the fact that teachers and their adolescent students do not spend the entire day together. In elementary school classrooms, teachers integrate their reading and writing instruction while teaching content. Although specific periods of the day are set aside for reading and language arts in elementary school, the focus and strategies used throughout the day and curriculum and can be more cohesive.

Does this mean that we would like to see middle and high school students with one teacher for the entire day? Certainly not! We know that middle and high school students need access to teachers who are passionate and knowledgeable about their respective subject areas. We also know that the texts students read across disciplines are more complex, and students often require instruction to access these texts. We do, however, believe that we can learn from the elementary school's ability to create an integrated experience for students.

In Chapter 2 we explore the role that teachers of the content areas (including science, music, math, art, social studies, and physical education) play in adolescent literacy. More specifically, we explore various instructional strategies that teachers and students can use to comprehend content. In addition, we explore the various types of texts that students can and should be reading, and the ways in which teachers can organize their instruction.

However, in this chapter we focus on English teachers. We know that English teachers can improve literacy achievement and that they can do so while addressing their specific content standards. We also know that they cannot create literate students alone and that they must collaborate with their content area colleagues to be successful. The essential question that guides our thinking about English teachers is this:

*Are students' reading and writing development and relevant life experiences used to explore literary concepts?*

As you read in the Overture, we have identified five major areas that support this essential question. In the sections that follow in this chapter we explore each of these in turn as we consider the role that English teachers can play in improving adolescent literacy and learning. Following this chapter we explore the ways in which content teachers can improve adolescent literacy and learning. We do not believe that English teachers can serve only as literature teachers. As Slater (2004) notes,

> The study of literature permeates the English classroom to such an extent that one begins to believe that the purpose and function of English instruction in America is to train the next generation of literary scholars rather than to provide an increasingly diverse student population with a knowledge base and strategies necessary to help all students achieve the compelling goal of high literacy. (p. 40)

## A Focus on Themes

We'll start by challenging a tradition of the English classroom—the whole-class novel. This one-size-fits-all approach to the curriculum does not respond to the unique needs, strengths, or interests of adolescents. Frankly, it does not work in reaching the goal of improving literacy achievement and creating lifelong learners and readers.

**AREA 1: ENGLISH LANGUAGE ARTS CLASS**
*1. Are students' reading and writing development and relevant life experiences used to explore literary concepts?*

|  | 5 | 4 | 3 | 2 | 1 |
|---|---|---|---|---|---|
| 1.1. Universal themes are the focus, as opposed to individual texts. | Multiple texts are used that allow students to explore big ideas such as life and death, what it means to be human, or survival. |  | One or two class texts are used and are based on an overall theme or question. |  | One whole-class novel is used. |

Imagine this English classroom. All the students are sitting in rows with their copies of *Romeo and Juliet* open. Their teacher reads aloud. After a few minutes, the teacher calls on a student who begins to read where the teacher left off. Once the student has read the page, he calls on more students until they have read for 25 minutes. At this point the teacher turns on the TV and the class watches a video of the section of the book they've just read—another 15 minutes. As the video catches up to where the class stopped reading, the teacher distributes a worksheet with a series of questions for the students to answer, like those shown in Figure 1.1.

So many things in this example are problematic. First, we know that round-robin, cold reading aloud is not effective (Optiz & Rasinski, 1998). Some have even called it educational malpractice (Fisher, Lapp, & Flood, 2005). Once a student has read an assigned section, what is the motivation to pay attention? After all, what are the chances that a student will be called on twice during the same period? If students detect a pattern in terms of who is called upon to read, they will likely read ahead and practice their part and not pay attention to what is being read aloud. And can you blame them? All

---

**FIGURE 1.1**
***Romeo and Juliet* Worksheet**

**Write TRUE or FALSE in the blank.**

_____  1. Romeo asked Juliet to marry him.

_____  2. "Wherefore art thou Romeo?" means "Where are you, Romeo?"

_____  3. "Titan's fiery wheels" is an allusion to the sun chariot from mythology.

_____  4. The friar's knowledge of herbs serves as a foreshadowing.

_____  5. Tybalt killed the prince's cousin.

_____  6. Mercutio and the nurse provide comic relief in the play.

_____  7. Romeo went to Mantua to live in exile.

_____  8. Friar Laurence comforts Romeo when he is crying over his banishment.

_____  9. Mercutio defends Romeo against Tybalt's insults.

_____ 10. The nurse comforts Juliet when her father says she must marry Paris.

they want to do is sound good in front of their peers. Unfortunately, this comes at the expense of comprehension. When poorer readers are selected to read aloud, the entire class has to listen to choppy reading that does not help improve anyone's fluency or comprehension. For the struggling reader, this experience is torturous. Students who find reading difficult will find any excuse to leave the classroom and hope that their absence is not noticed upon their return (see Mooney & Cole, 2000).

Second, we know that students think about texts according to the ways they are questioned about the text (Anderson & Biddle, 1975; Hansen, 1981). Students reading *Romeo and Juliet* in the way described in this scenario will likely focus on the details of the play and miss the major ideas. As they read—or listen, as the case may be—they will focus on minutia at the expense of thinking.

Third, the structure of the classroom did not provide for student engagement. Rather, students sat passively while listening to the text. Listening isn't the problem here. We know that read-alouds are a powerful way of engaging students (see Ivey, 2003). The problem is that the students didn't *do* anything with the text. Read-alouds need to be interactive. In their study of interactive read-alouds, Fisher, Flood, Lapp, and Frey (2004) identified seven factors for effective read-alouds, including:

• The read-aloud text was selected based on the interests and needs of the students as well as the content covered.
• The selection was reviewed and practiced by the teacher.
• A clear purpose for the read-aloud was established.
• The teacher modeled fluent reading.
• The teacher was animated and expressive during the read-aloud.
• Students discussed the text during and after the read-aloud.
• The read-aloud was connected to other reading and united events in the classroom.

Finally, and most important, this classroom did not provide students with opportunities to select books that were interesting and that they could read. "Getting through the content" is one goal, and the *Romeo and Juliet* unit of study based on a whole-class novel could be improved such that every student understood the plot, character development, setting, and other components of the story grammar. That still would not result in better readers

---

FIGURE 1.2
**Examples of Big Ideas and Essential Questions**

- If we can, should we?
- What does it mean to be human?
- Man versus machine
- The hero in literature
- Man versus himself
- What should a city provide its citizens?
- What makes democracy?
- Power to the people

---

and writers who read and write more—a goal that we believe must always complement the units of study in an English class.

So what might be an alternative? A better way to organize this curriculum might be around a theme, a big idea, or an essential question (see Jorgensen, 1994–1995). Some examples of big ideas and essential questions appear in Figure 1.2 (see above). The teacher from the *Romeo and Juliet* scenario might have selected the idea "Love, Life, and Death" as a way to organize instruction. In doing so, he might have asked students to read different texts and to write about their personal experiences and interactions they had with the texts.

Although organizing instruction around a theme, a big idea, or an essential question might be an improvement, text selection plays an important—critical, in fact—role in what students will learn. Let's focus next on the texts that can, and should, be used in an English class that is well organized.

## Text Difficulty

| AREA 1: ENGLISH LANGUAGE ARTS CLASS | | | | | |
|---|---|---|---|---|---|
| *1. Are students' reading and writing development and relevant life experiences used to explore literary concepts?* | | | | | |
| | **5** | **4** | **3** | **2** | **1** |
| 1.2. Selected texts span a range of difficulty levels. | Multiple texts are used, and students select texts based on their interests and reading levels. | | An alternative is identified for struggling readers, or book clubs require forced choices. | | Grade-level texts are used. |

Think about the English class that is organized around the idea of "Love, Life, and Death." It would not be much of a stretch to invite students to select one of the following books: *West Side Story* (Shulman, 1961) *Romiette and Julio* (Draper, 2001), or *Romeo and Juliet Together (and Alive!) at Last* (Avi, 1988). In this situation, students may be reading in small groups and discussing their books with groups of peers. These book clubs or literature circles add a level of engagement and discussion as students work in their groups (Daniels, 2002). Typically during these small-group discussions, students are assigned roles such as "discussion director" or "timekeeper." In addition, students may be assigned any of the following roles (Frey & Fisher, 2006, p. 133):

• *Literary Luminary*—chooses passages for discussion and formulates theories on their importance in the story.

• *Connector*—makes connections between events or characters in the book and personal experiences, other books, or events in the world.

• *Illustrator*—creates a sketch, graph, flow chart, or diagram to portray a topic for discussion.

• *Summarizer*—composes a statement that captures the main idea of the reading.

• *Vocabulary Enricher*—locates important words and provides a definition for the group.

• *Researcher*—investigates background information that is key to understanding the reading.

Although this approach is an improvement over the whole-class novel or another "grade-level" text, a teacher can do even more to engage students with texts. You probably noticed that the texts selected for discussion were all closely tied to *Romeo and Juliet*. As such, the choices were limited and the theme was constrained by someone's need to select texts that provided students with *Romeo and Juliet* in a lighter version. Some teachers who use this approach secretly pine away at the loss of *Romeo and Juliet* and hope that they will, some day, teach advanced placement or gifted students so that they can bring this classic back into the classroom.

If it sounds as though we hate Shakespeare, that isn't the case. Shakespeare and other works from the canon of great literature can and should be part of the English curriculum. We just know that texts have to be matched to students. We have a hard time imagining a 9th grade class of 36 students all reading, and willing to read, the same book at the same time.

Returning to the big idea that guided the selection of these books, "Love, Life, and Death," we suggest expanding the selection of texts even further. Students thinking about the big idea may be concerned about issues of suicide, relationship violence, peer pressure, and family influence. Figure 1.3 contains a list of adolescent fiction that expands the exploration of the big idea into very different directions.

As you may have guessed, text selection is complex. There are so many good books to choose from and so little time! That's why we are concerned about selecting texts—time is limited, and it is wasted when students are not reading.

---

### FIGURE 1.3
### Books to Consider for the Big Idea of "Love, Life, and Death"

**Suicide**

Crutcher, C. (1991). *Chinese handcuffs*. New York: Laurel Leaf.
Draper, S. M. (1996). *Tears of a tiger*. New York: Simon Pulse.
Fields, T. (2002). *After the death of Anna Gonzales*. New York: Henry Holt & Company.
Fleischman, P. (1998). *Whirligig*. New York: Laurel Leaf.
Frank, E. R. (2000). *Life is funny*. New York: Dorling Kindersley Publishing.
Frank, E. R. (2002). *America*. New York: Simon Pulse.
Runyon, B. (2004). *The burn journals*. New York: Alfred A. Knopf.

**Relationship Violence**

Dessen, S. (2000). *Dreamland*. New York: Speak.
Flinn, A. (2002). *Breathing underwater*. New York: HarperTempest.
Miklowitz, G. D. (1995). *Past forgiving*. New York: Simon & Schuster.
Tashjian, J. (2003). *Fault line*. New York: Henry Holt & Company.

**Peer Pressure**

Atkins, C. (2003). *Alt ed*. New York: G. P. Putnam's Sons.
Hartinger, B. (2003). *Geography club*. New York: HarperTempest.
Wittlinger, E. (2001). *Hard love*. New York: Simon Pulse.
Wittlinger, E. (2001). *Razzle*. New York: Simon Pulse.

**Family Influence**

Ellis, D. (2000). *The breadwinner*. Toronto: Groundwood.
Peters, J. A. (2004). *Luna*. New York: Little Brown & Company.
Trueman, T. (2000). *Stuck in neutral*. New York: HarperCollins.

Not only do we want books that are aligned with a theme, a big idea, or an essential question, we also need books that students can read. Text difficulty is an important consideration in text selection. One factor to consider is the book's readability. Readability is fairly easy to determine, using one of two common methods: the Fry Readability Rating or the Flesch Reading Ease Score and Flesch-Kincaid Grade Level Score.

## Fry Readability

A Fry Readability Rating can be calculated using the graph in Figure 1.4 and these simple steps:

1. Select three 100-word passages from the book, preferably one each from the beginning, middle, and end.

2. Count the number of sentences in each passage and the number of syllables in each passage.

3. Average each of the two factors (number of sentences and number of syllables), then plot the result on the graph.

This will yield an approximate grade level.

## Flesch Reading Ease Score and Flesch-Kincaid Grade Level Score

Most word-processing software programs have a feature for determining text difficulty. Simply type in a passage from a book you would like to assess, and then run the calculation. For example, the Microsoft Word program computes a Flesch Reading Ease Score on a 100-point scale. On this scale, the higher the score, the easier the text is to read. This software program also reports a Flesch-Kincaid Grade Level Score to approximate difficulty.

To run these calculations on Microsoft Word, go to "Tools" on the toolbar and select "Spelling and Grammar." After running the spell check for the document, click on "Options" and check "Show readability formulas." After clicking OK, the program will report both scores. The Flesch Reading Ease Score for this section was a moderately difficult 56.1 and the Flesch-Kincaid Grade Level Score was 9.5.

Although readability formulas can be helpful, they cannot select books for students. In some cases, the content of the book is not consistent with the reading level at which the book was written. For example, a Flesch-Kincaid Grade Level analysis of a section of *Cat's Cradle* by Kurt Vonnegut (1998), a satire of a world on the edge of an apocalypse, revealed a level score of 2.3. If

## FIGURE 1.4
## Fry Readability Graph

**Graph for estimating readability—extended
by Edward Fry**

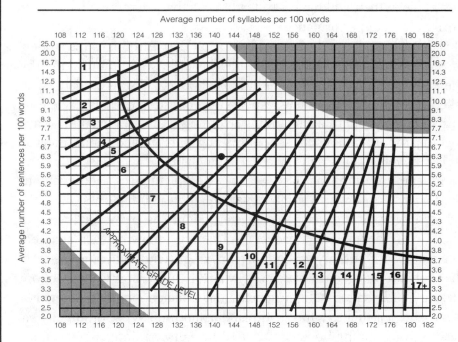

Directions: Randomly select 3 one hundred word passages from a book or an article. Plot average number of syllables and average number of sentences per 100 words on graph to determine the grade level of the material. Choose more passages per book if great variability is observed and conclude that the book has uneven readability. Few books will fall in gray area but when they do grade level scores are invalid.

Count proper nouns, numerals, and initialization as words. Count a syllable for each symbol. For example, "1945" is 1 word and 4 syllables and "IRA" is 1 word and 3 syllables.

| Example: | Syllables | Sentences |
|---|---|---|
| First hundred words | 124 | 6.6 |
| Second hundred words | 141 | 5.5 |
| Third hundred words | 158 | 6.8 |
| Average | 141 | 6.3 |

Readability seventh grade (see dot plotted on graph)

*Source:* Fry, E. B. (1968, April). A readability formula that saves time. *Journal of Reading, 11*(7), 513–516. Reprinted with permission.

you've read this book, you know it would hardly be appropriate for 2nd graders. Although this example may be an outlier, it does highlight the need for teachers and students to be the ones selecting texts. Szymusiak and Sibberson (2001) remind us that we have to think beyond "leveled books" based on readability alone and acknowledge that students' interests and motivation also play a role in their willingness to read books that are more difficult than their current level of performance.

Consider the student who reads nothing all day. Although this student may or may not be able to read, the student is clearly communicating this message: "This reading thing doesn't have *me* hooked." If this student's parents asked about school, the likely response to a question such as, "What did you learn today?" would be a resounding "Nothing!" Take, for example, Cary, a 10th grader whose options for school reading were limited to the assigned whole-class novels in his English class. His English teacher constantly complained in team meetings that Cary was not completing the accompanying activities for this novel, which students were reading aloud in class (the activities included a graphic organizer on characterization, a list of vocabulary words from the book to define, and a packet of questions following each chapter). In fact, it was clear that Cary was not even paying attention during the reading. The problem was that the class novel was too difficult for Cary to follow, and hearing his classmates take turns reading, some choppy and others in a monotone, did nothing to support his understanding. What did finally get Cary reading was finding books that suited his personal interests and more closely matched his reading level? Cary's interest in the Civil War inspired his teacher to begin reading the historical fiction novel *Bull Run* (Fleischman, 1993) with him. He finished this book on his own and, with his teacher's help, located two additional historical novels on the topic, *Across the Lines* (Reeder, 1997) and *Joseph: 1861—Rumble of War* (Pryor, 1999), and, a nonfiction selection, *A Day That Changed America: Gettysburg* (Tanaka, 2003). He read these books cover to cover, with no prodding. If we focus on themes or big ideas, rather than specific books, we can make reading more possible and more appealing to students like Cary (and there are lots of Carys out there).

Let us emphasize this again—the materials and instructional routines used in the English classroom must engage the adolescent learner. Whole-class novels are unlikely to do so. Similarly, books that are not interesting or are too difficult will not engage students. So far, we have focused our conversation on using themes, big ideas, or essential questions; multiple texts; and texts that students want to and can read. We now take a broader focus—one that requires that the first two issues be considered in the context of the adolescent learner.

## Selecting Instructional Materials

| AREA 1: ENGLISH LANGUAGE ARTS CLASS<br>1. Are students' reading and writing development and relevant life experiences used to explore literary concepts? | | | | | | | | |
|---|---|---|---|---|---|---|---|---|
| | **5** | **4** | **3** | **2** | **1** |
| 1.3. Reading and writing instruction and materials address contemporary and engaging issues. | Current adolescent literature and infor mational texts, including electronic formats, are featured prominently. Writing is used for multiple purposes, and students write across genres. | | Classics are supplemented with contemporary readings; writing is used as a way for students to communicate, and students write for multiple purposes. | | Only classics are read, and writing is limited to traditional forms such as the five-paragraph essay. |

With the caveat that each learner is exceptional and brings a unique range of background knowledge and prior experiences to the learning environment, we hope that classrooms address contemporary, relevant, and interesting issues. In other words, we hope that the themes, big ideas, or essential questions used to guide the curriculum are not ones that will bore students to tears. Maybe we should have said this before, but not all themes, big ideas, and essential questions are created equal. Imagine spending six weeks focusing on a question such as "What does Wadsworth mean?" or the theme "Weather." Those topics would not be likely to engage today's students.

So how does a busy English teacher find topics that engage adolescents? Ask them! We predict that students will have lots of individual interests and some common ones. The common interests, obtained through an interest inventory or similar tool, can be fodder for organizing instruction.

While we acknowledge that most English teachers want to (make that *love* to) teach literature, at least four reasons justify increasing the amount of

---

**FIGURE 1.5**
**Informational Books That Can Serve as Models for Writing**

Armstrong, J. (2000). *Theodore Roosevelt: Letters from a young coal miner*. New York: Winslow. (*Letters*)

Bolden, T. (2001). *Tell all the children our story: Memories and mementos of being young and black in America*. New York: Harry N. Abrams. (*Memoir*)

King, M. L. (1997). *I have a dream*. New York: Scholastic. (*Speech*)

Langley, A., & De Souza, P. (1996). *The Roman news*. Cambridge, MA: Candlewick. (*Newspaper*)

Leedy, L. (1996). *Postcards from Pluto: A tour of the solar system*. New York: Holiday House. (*Postcards*)

Talbott, H. (2003). *Safari journal: The adventures in Africa of Carey Monroe*. New York: Silver Whistle. (*Journal*)

Tunnell, M. O. (1996). *The children of Topaz: The story of a Japanese-American internment camp*. New York: Holiday House. (*Diary*)

Wright-Frierson, V. (1998). *A desert scrapbook: Dawn to dusk in the Sonoran Desert*. New York: Aladdin. (*Scrapbook*)

---

informational texts used in the classroom. First, lots of students love informational texts, and some of these students aren't into narrative texts, fiction, or stories. Second, informational texts permeate our lives outside school. Students will read for information in many ways, both at home and at work, so it's important that they be guided and taught to comprehend these books. Third, informational texts provide excellent models for the kinds of writing students might experiment with outside school (see Figure 1.5 above for a list of informational texts used as models for writing). And fourth, if we haven't convinced you yet, use informational texts because the standards say so.

## Instruction That Builds Competence

| AREA 1: ENGLISH LANGUAGE ARTS CLASS<br>1. *Are students' reading and writing development and relevant life experiences used to explore literary concepts?* | | | | | |
|---|---|---|---|---|---|
| | **5** | **4** | **3** | **2** | **1** |
| 1.4. Instruction builds students' reading and writing competence. | A gradual release of responsibility guides the teachers' instruction and results in increased achievement. | | Groups of students work on skill assignments that are related to the theme. | | Skill work is assigned and may appear remedial in nature. |

Literacy—reading, writing, speaking, listening, and viewing—is a developmental process, and literacy skills develop along a continuum (Flood, Lapp, Squire, & Jensen, 2003; Squire, 1987; Tinajero & Ada, 1993). Every student is someplace on the literacy continuum, and as Farnan, Flood, and Lapp (1994) note, "There is no point on the continuum that denotes too much literacy or, for that matter, not enough. There are no good or bad places to be, only places informed by children's previous knowledge and construction of literacy concepts." (p. 136)

What, then, should the English teacher do? If every student in the class is at a different development point on the literacy continuum, how can the classroom be structured to ensure that students learn the content while developing their literacy skills? Given this, can you see why the whole-class-novel approach simply does not work?

The most promising answer to these questions at this time is the "gradual release of responsibility" model (Pearson & Fielding, 1991). In this model, teachers move from assuming "all the responsibility for performing a task . . . to a situation in which students assume all of the responsibility" (Duke & Pearson, 2002, p. 211). Teachers begin with explicit instruction in a skill or strategy. Over time, guided instruction allows students to try the skills or strategies for themselves. Students gradually assume more responsibility for using the skill or strategy as they work with one another as well as independently.

Fisher and Frey (2003) examined the ways in which a gradual-release-of-responsibility model might improve the writing achievement of struggling adolescent readers. Their work suggests that teachers can gradually release responsibility for writing by using varied instructional approaches. It is important to note that all students—or all classes, for that matter—do not start at the same point in the model. The starting point is determined by student performance data and the goals of instruction. For a writing curriculum, a gradual release of responsibility might include the language experience approach, interactive writing, writing models, generative sentences, power writing, and independent writing prompts with rubrics.

## Language Experience Approach (LEA)

The language experience approach dates back at least 40 years (Ashton-Warner, 1959; Dixon & Nessel, 1983). LEA makes the "speech to print" connection clear to students by inviting them to have a conversation. As part of the conversation, they agree on specific sentences that capture their thinking. The teacher writes these sentences on the dry-erase board, chart paper, or overhead transparency, allowing students the experience of the discussion and writing, while the full responsibility for writing is the teacher's.

## Interactive Writing

Although interactive writing has its roots in teaching young writers (McCarrier, Pinnell, & Fountas, 2000), we know that it is also effective with adolescents (Fisher & Frey, 2003). Interactive writing can be used with either the whole class or with small groups. The idea is to engage students in relevant conversations, help them record these conversations, and provide instruction in the purposes and conventions of writing. Similar to the language experience approach, interactive writing moves "from ideas, to spoken words, to printed messages" (Clay, 2001, p. 27). Instruction begins with a conversation. Students then agree upon a sentence or two to record. The difference between LEA and interactive writing is in who does the writing. In interactive writing, students are invited to the overhead, chart paper, or dry-erase board to write. Students do *not* write the entire message; rather, they write individual words or phrases and share the pen with one another. As students take turns writing, the teacher provides instruction on language structure or function based on the word or phrase being written. This instruction ranges from word families to grammar to conventions of writing. Whereas 5- and 6-year-olds are very excited to get the chance to write, we know that adolescents require a bit more encouragement and trust to begin.

## Writing Models

Consistent with the gradual-release-of-responsibility model, writing models further reduce the role of the teacher in writing. As we saw in LEA, the teacher did all the writing. During interactive writing, students did more of the writing but had the support of an agreed-upon message. Using existing writing as a model for new writing is another step in the gradual release. As modeled in the popular film *Finding Forrester* (Wolf, King, & Van Sant, 2000), students can begin with previously published writing. "I am" poems, such as the one in Figure 1.6, are a popular writing model and are especially useful in character analysis.

---

**FIGURE 1.6**
**Stanzas for an "I Am" Poem**

---

I am (special characteristics or nouns about you).
I wonder (something you are curious about).
I hear (an imaginary sound).
I want (an actual desire of yours).
I am (repeat first line of poem).
I pretend (something you pretend to do).
I feel (an imaginary feeling).
I touch (an imaginary touch).
I worry (something that truly bothers you).
I cry (something that makes you very sad).
I am (repeat the first line of the poem).
I understand (something you know is true).
I say (something that you believe in).
I dream (something you dream about).
I try (something you make an effort about).
I hope (something you actually hope for).
I am (repeat the first line of the poem).

---

Picture books also provide great writing models. For example, *Martin's Big Words* (Rappaport, 2001) incorporates lines from Dr. Martin Luther King Jr.'s speeches to explain the history of the time. Students can use this model, the incorporation of published speeches, to write their own historical accounts.

Another type of writing model is called a "paragraph frame." Teachers can easily create paragraph frames by starting sentences with phrases that include ellipses. For example, related to the theme "Love, Life, and Death," students might be asked to complete the following: "When I think of love . . ." or "Love is . . ." Other possibilities are "Life is . . ." or "To love life . . ." At each of the ellipses, students add their own text. As a result, students have more responsibility for the writing and the teacher has less.

## Generative Sentences

Building on the practice of a "given word sentence" (Fearn & Farnan, 2001, p. 87), generative sentences increase the amount of responsibility students have and allow teachers to focus on the craft of writing. Although teachers can use generative sentences in many ways, the idea is to provide students with a word and the placement in a sentence for that word. For example, a teacher may ask students to "write a sentence with the word *love* in the fourth position." Following the construction of the sentence, the teacher can ask students to generate a paragraph, a poem, or an essay based on their sentence.

Some of the variations of generative writing include focusing on words students confuse (e.g., *there, their, they're*); asking students to use the word in different positions in different sentences (e.g., write four sentences, using *life* in the first, second, third, and final positions); or asking them to write sentences with designated numbers of words (e.g., write a sentence of at least eight words with *death* in the fourth position; write a sentence of no more than seven words with *love* in the final position).

Regardless of how generative sentences are used, the idea is to release additional responsibility to students by just providing them with the word and a position for the word. Using generative sentences, each student's sentence should be unique. This allows the teacher to assess grammar and vocabulary knowledge and plan instruction accordingly.

## Power Writing

As students progress in their writing skills, they will need to learn to write more. Although reading fluency has received a great deal of attention, writing fluency is often neglected. Power writing is a fluency activity, "a structured free-write where the objective is quantity alone" (Fearn & Farnan, 2001, p. 501). The idea is for students to write as many words as they can as fast as they can. The instructional sequence for power writing is quite simple. Students are given a prompt and timed for one minute. The teacher typically says, "Write as much as you can, as well as you can." As the timer rings, students are reminded to "count your number of words and circle any words that you think are incorrect."

Following three one-minute rounds, often with different topics, students graph their highest score (see Kasper-Ferguson & Moxley, 2002). Power writing releases further responsibility to students in that they are provided only with a general topic and a set amount of time. Students compete against themselves, not other members of the class, with the goal of increasing their fluency. Power writing also provides students with self-created material to revise.

In addition, power writing provides teachers with assessment information that they can use in planning instruction. We all make mistakes when we write, especially when we write quickly. An important fact is that we notice these mistakes when we reread our work. Teachers using power writing as an assessment tool do not worry about the mistakes that students notice in their writing, but they do pay attention to the mistakes that their students do not notice.

## Independent Writing Prompts with Rubrics

Independent writing is the ultimate goal of our gradual release of responsibility in writing instruction. It's important to say this: We don't use this model so that students become good at interactive writing or using writing models. We do this so that students can write for a variety of purposes, including responding to a prompt. As Carol Jago (2002, p. 15) notes, "Teachers must strike a balance between giving students too much and too little choice in writing prompts."

We know that simply assigning writing—causing writing—rather than teaching writing is not helpful and violates the concept of a gradual release of responsibility. Students must know what is expected of them and believe that they can accomplish it. Writing rubrics, especially rubrics that are developed with students, provide students with clear expectations and guidance as they respond to prompts. We have found a Web-based rubric creation system, rubistar.4teachers.org, helpful in creating writing rubrics with students.

## Gradual Release of Responsibility in Reading

For reading instruction, one way to think about the gradual-release-of-responsibility model is in terms of classroom organization and structure. Reading strategies and skills can be introduced to the whole class, practiced with small groups, and then reinforced with individual students.

A typical class session may be organized into the following activities (Frey & Fisher, 2007). The first 5 to 15 minutes are devoted to a *focus lesson*. The idea of the focus lesson is to provide students with instruction in a specific skill or strategy based on a piece of text. Focus lessons could consist of minilessons, a maxilesson, shared reading, shared writing, or think-alouds (see Allen, 2000; Calkins, 2001; Fearn & Farnan, 2001; Wilhelm, 2001). The point is to model what good readers do and to provide students with explicit instruction. Every piece of text could be used for a host of different purposes; the key to the focus lesson is establishing a specific purpose with students.

Next, the teacher meets with one or two small groups of students per day for 10 to 20 minutes for *guided instruction*. Students in these groups are selected based on similar needs or interests, and groups range from two to five students.

During this time, the teacher may follow up with another reading with the same purpose as the focus lesson or may provide some assessment-driven instruction such as word study, making meaning, strategy use, or understanding literary devices (to name a few). Regardless, the guided instruction should be tailored to the needs of the students in the group.

While the teacher meets with the guided-instruction group, the rest of the class is engaged in *collaborative learning*. Collaborative learning requires that all students work with at least one other person; the groups can become as large as five members. The key is to provide students with meaningful and relevant activities that are connected with the content and purpose established earlier.

As guided instruction and collaborative learning rotations come to an end, students work for 25 minutes on *independent reading*. While students read independently, the teacher meets with individual students to confer and assess reading. The point of the independent reading is to use the skills and strategies acquired over the term with books that students can read by themselves. (In Chapter 3 we also explore how free voluntary reading, such as Sustained Silent Reading, can be used with adolescents.)

Much like the gradual release of responsibility in writing instruction, the structure of reading instruction must provide for individual differences and must ensure that students have access to models before being expected to perform skills and strategies on their own.

## Teaching Students to Understand Literature and Literary Devices

| AREA 1: ENGLISH LANGUAGE ARTS CLASS<br>1. Are students' reading and writing development and relevant life experiences used to explore literary concepts? | | | | | | |
|---|---|---|---|---|---|---|
| | **5** | **4** | **3** | **2** | **1** |
| 1.5. Literary devices are taught with texts that are readable and meaningful to students. | Literary devices are studied across texts and genres before students experiment with these devices in their writing. | | Literary devices are taught out of context or with texts that are too difficult for students to understand; students are not expected to write using these devices. | | Literary devices are taught as vocabulary terms to be memorized. |

As you may have noticed by now, we believe that English teachers must develop their students' literacy skills. We have noted that English classrooms should be organized around big ideas, that these big ideas should matter and be relevant to students, and that instruction should follow a gradual-release-of-responsibility model to ensure that all students progress along the continuum of literacy and language acquisition.

We also know that an entire curriculum is assigned to English teachers and that their job is not easy. In addition to developing and extending each student's literacy skills, English teachers must ensure that students develop their skills of literary analysis. This does not mean that English teachers have to use whole-class novels to do so. Let's stop by Ms. Javier's classroom and listen in on her focus lesson.

The purpose of her lesson is to facilitate students' understanding of tone—how to read for tone, how to recognize changes in tone, and how authors use words to establish tone. An important point is that the focus on tone was not the overall theme, big idea, or essential question that guided the inquiry of this group of students. Instead, the students were all focused on "What's worth fighting for?" as their essential question.

Think about the ways that Ms. Javier might focus on tone (a literary device that the state standards require to be taught). She might give students a definition for tone, such as this:

> The attitude an author takes toward a subject or character—such as hateful, serious, humorous, sarcastic, solemn, objective—conveys the tone or mood. The author can use dialogue, settings, or descriptions to set a tone or mood.

Does testing students' understanding of this definition help them read and write better? Simply testing the definition probably won't even help students on the state standardized test—if they remember the definition that long. Most standards-aligned assessments require that students *use* the information, not just regurgitate it.

Could Ms. Javier use a grade-level text or whole-class novel to teach her students about tone? Of course she could, but that would violate our earlier discussions about text selections and gradual release of responsibility. It seems reasonable to suggest that the text difficulty should be reduced when introducing new vocabulary and concepts. That's not rocket science, but it's important.

The students in Ms. Javier's class had been engaged with the essential question for several weeks, reading widely on the topic and writing in response to their readings and to prompts suggested by Ms. Javier and other students in the class. Ms. Javier used her focus-lesson time to select texts and provide instruction on literary devices. Her students had become accustomed to reading along with her with their eyes as she read aloud. They also knew that they would stop periodically and discuss the text and write about it.

As the class begins, the students notice that Ms. Javier has projected the picture book *Faithful Elephants* (Tsuchiya, 1988) on the screen, using a document camera. She reminds her students that authors use words to set a tone and that the tone is something that readers infer, not something that the author says directly. Before beginning she reviews examples of phrases found in other books and the tones they represent.

Ms. Javier reads the first page, in which cherry blossoms are blooming and people are visiting a zoo. The illustration suggests that the story is set in Japan. Ms. Javier says, "All these things—the cherry trees, the blooms, the soft breeze, sparkling petals, and a beautiful day—make me think this is a hopeful story. I like the tone—it's hopeful. People are out visiting the zoo on a wonderful spring day."

She reads again, noting that her students should keep their eyes and ears ready for changes in the tone. After a few more pages, she pauses. Readers have just found out that three elephants used to live at this zoo while Japan was at war. People were worried that bombs might fall on the zoo and that the animals would escape into the city. Through her discussion with the students and their selection of specific words, they decide that the tone has changed to fear.

This process continues, and the readers learn that the elephants were killed, starved to death, while Japan was bombed during World War II. Several shifts in tone occur; *hope, fear, resignation, love, tragedy, mourning, anger,* and *resolution* are all words the students use to describe various points in the text. Each student has a two-column journal. In their journals, the students identify the changes in tone in the left column and the author's words that led them to identify the tone in the right column.

As the focus lesson comes to an end, Ms. Javier, with tears in her eyes, asks her students, "What's worth fighting for?" Her students will remember this lesson for so many reasons—their teacher cried, defenseless animals died, and they were engaged, like detectives, in finding out how an author of a book they could read and wanted to read used words to set a tone.

You see, literary devices are important tools that authors use to help readers. Students need to be able to identify these devices and use them in their own writing. We wholeheartedly support a focus on literary devices and responding to literature. Our argument is with the way these devices are too often taught—out of context or with books that students simply do not care about.

✱ ✱ ✱ ✱ ✱

Now that you've read this chapter, you have a sense of what we think makes up a high-quality English classroom. You may disagree with us on some of the points. Great! Conversations about what is possible and what we can expect are important. But we encourage you to take a minute and reflect. If you scored yourself on the rubrics for this chapter, how did you do? How would your colleagues do? What professional development would be required to move people forward in their ability to provide an English curriculum and class in this way? What resources might be available and useful?

Having considered the answers to these questions, we move beyond the English classroom. Improving adolescent literacy is a schoolwide responsibility and does not rest on the shoulders of the English department alone. As you will see, there are specific ways that all teachers can use reading, writing, speaking, listening, and viewing to ensure that their students learn the content. Along the way, if done well, all students' literacy achievement will improve.

Remember, there is no good or bad place for students to be on the literacy continuum as long as they are moving forward and reading and writing more and better all of the time. This goes for students who read at or above grade level as well—they, too, can improve their performance. Unfortunately, some students lose ground in their literacy development—a situation that is almost always preventable with good teaching. We hope we've inspired you to read further.

# 2

## Transportable and Transparent Strategies for Content Literacy Instruction

As we noted in Chapter 1, English teachers have a significant role to play in the literacy achievement of secondary school students. However, they are not alone in this effort. Every content teacher has a role to play if adolescents are to learn with and from texts. Further, students must be able to read a wide variety of texts, from great works of literature to newspaper articles to technical manuals to science lab instructions. To do this, students require instruction and practice in reading these types of materials. As we have noted before, all learning is language based. We all learn by reading, writing, speaking, listening, and viewing. Each component of literacy must be taught and used across the school day. When this happens, the strategies we teach become transportable and transparent for students.

By *transportable,* we mean that students use the strategies they learn in one class to comprehend in another. By *transparent,* we mean that strategies become part of the students' thinking, and students automatically apply the strategies "on the run." When strategies become transportable and transparent, students focus more on the content being taught than on how they are being taught. To explore this idea in greater depth, we look at a high school student and learn about his experiences with literacy across the content areas. Then we explore a school in which teachers consistently use literacy instructional strategies. We conclude this chapter with a discussion of the texts and ideas that can be used to organize instruction. By the end of the chapter, you'll be able to answer our essential question:

*Do all courses throughout a student's day capitalize on the student's literacy and language as a way to learn new information?*

## Abdurashid's Story

Abdurashid Ali is an immigrant from Ethiopia. When he arrived in the United States, in the middle of his freshman year, he spoke four languages: Oromo, Amharic, Swahili, and Somali. He did not speak English and had lived in a Kenyan refugee camp for the four years preceding his arrival into the United States. As a senior, he had to move into his own apartment because his father demanded that he quit school and work full-time or move out. Abdurashid did not want to quit school; he wanted to continue to learn, to get a college education, and to help his family in more significant ways when he finished school. In response to a question about the importance of education, Abdurashid wrote the following in an e-mail message:

> Well, starting life in US was as hard as it gets when I first got here. We had to start every-thing from skratch. Adapt to a new culture, life style, language and people. From this you can tell that I needed guidance or someone who could help me learn about this new life, the language, and everything I needed to survive in my new home. The perfect place for this was school. In past five years, prior to my arrival to the US, I was unable to go to school. And ever since I started school back home, I loved going to school and valued education. So, losing my education was like giving away something I valued the most.

During his senior year, Abdurashid received letters of acceptance from several colleges. He chose to attend the University of California at San Diego and study premedicine. His goal is to become a cardiologist. We believe that there are many lessons to learn from this particular student—a student who knew no English in 9th grade but who completed AP English, AP Physics, Algebra II, government, economics, and art during his senior year.

## Using Big Ideas or Themes

Observing Abdurashid in class reveals important lessons about content area literacy. His school operates on a four-by-four block schedule, meaning that all students take three or four classes in the fall and then three or four classes in the spring. During the spring term of his senior year, he started his day in AP Physics. The unit of study that the physics class was

| AREA 2: CONTENT AREA CLASSES 2. Do all courses throughout a student's day capitalize on the student's literacy and language as a way to learn new information? | | | | | | | | |
|---|---|---|---|---|---|---|---|---|
| | **5** | | **4** | | **3** | | **2** | **I** |
| **2.1. Big ideas are the focus of students' reading and writing** | Students construct knowledge by connecting new knowledge with prior knowledge and relevant life experiences in all of their reading and writing. | | | | Students read about big ideas, or themes are presented; yet assessments focus on discrete knowledge and facts. | | | Reading and writing focus on discrete knowledge and skills; students are expected to memorize facts. |

engaged with was based on a theme called "Sounds Like Fun!" Like the English classes described in Chapter 1, content area classrooms should be organized around themes, big ideas, or essential questions.

## Daily Reading and Writing

| AREA 2: CONTENT AREA CLASSES 2. Do all courses throughout a student's day capitalize on the student's literacy and language as a way to learn new information? | | | | | | | | |
|---|---|---|---|---|---|---|---|---|
| | **5** | | **4** | | **3** | | **2** | **I** |
| **2.2. Students are expected to read and write in every class.** | Reading, writing, speaking, and listening are used throughout the period, and students have the opportunity to demonstrae their content understanding in multiple ways. | | | | Students read or write periodically and may be asked to demonstrate their undersanding through language. | | | Class instruction is lecture and recall or activity oriented; textbook reading is assigned for homework. |

Upon entering the physics room, students saw a writing-to-learn prompt on the board. Abdurashid immediately got to work responding to the prompt. On this particular day, the teacher used a RAFT prompt (Santa & Havens, 1995), which stands for:

R = role (Who is the writer, what is role of the writer?)
A = audience (To whom are you writing?)
F = format (What format should the writing be in?)
T = topic (What are you writing about?)

The teacher had written the following RAFT on the board:
R = sound wave
A = human ear
F = mobile phone conversation
T = Can you hear me? Can you hear me now?

The teacher then asked the students to respond to a series of questions in the format of an anticipation guide (see Head & Readence, 1986). The purpose is to activate prior knowledge, encourage predictions, and stimulate curiosity about a topic. Abdurashid responded to the questions in Figure 2.1.

Following the writing-to-learn and anticipatory activities, the teacher began discussing sound waves. He presented a series of graphic organizers demonstrating the ways in which sound travels and what happens when waves cross one another. As he did so, Abdurashid took notes using a Cornell

### FIGURE 2.1
### Anticipation Guide in a Physics Class

| Before Reading<br>A = Agree<br>D = Disagree | Statement | After Reading<br>A = Agree<br>D = Disagree |
|---|---|---|
| | Two notes that have a frequency ratio of 2:1 are said to be separated by an octave. | |
| | A sound wave is different from a light wave in that a sound wave is produced by an oscillating object and a light wave is not. | |
| | A sound wave is different from a light wave in that a sound wave is not capable of traveling through a vacuum. | |
| | A sound wave is different from a light wave in that a sound wave is capable of diffracting and a light wave is not. | |

note page (Pauk, 2000), writing main ideas and key words on the left side of the vertical line, details on the right, and a brief summary at the bottom. A sample Cornell note page appears in Figure 2.2.

The teacher also identified key vocabulary terms, including *wave, equilibrium, medium, frequency, mechanical waves,* and *electromagnetic waves.* He asked the students to create word cards to help them remember the words.

---

**FIGURE 2.2**
**Cornell Note Page**

| Name: _____ | Date: _____ | Class: _____ | Page: _____ |

| Main Ideas and Key Words | Details |
|---|---|
|  |  |
| Summary |  |

A word card has four quadrants divided into a 3-by-5-inch or 5-by-7-inch index card.

| Word | What the word means |
|------|---------------------|
| Illustration | What the word doesn't mean |

Later that period, the teacher read aloud a selection from *Light, Sound, and Waves Science Fair Projects: Using Sunglasses, Guitars, CDs, and Other Stuff* by Robert Gardner (2004) and then showed a short film about sound waves. During the film, Abdurashid took notes using his Cornell note pages.

During the passing period, we asked Abdurashid how he learned so much science while he was learning to speak, read, and write in English. He said, "The best way for me is the pictures." When asked what he meant by that, Abdurashid opened his notebook and showed us several graphic organizers and said, "Like this—the pictures Mr. Cox uses to teach." Looking through his notebook revealed several graphic organizers, including those he had copied from the teacher's presentation and graphic organizers he had created based on the lecture or reading material. When asked if he learned in other ways, Abdurashid said that he was good at taking notes. "I learned to take notes my first year here. They taught me how to make the paper so you could find information again." He showed us a page of notes from his history class that were organized in the Cornell note-taking format. As he entered his next class, Abdurashid said, "They have good teachers here. They make class interesting, and you want to learn. I wanted to know the right answers to those wave questions so I had to pay attention in class."

It is clear that the reason that Abdurashid did so well in his AP Physics class was related to the teacher. More specifically, it was the ways in which the teacher engaged the class and ensured that the physics content was accessible for the students. The teacher used evidence-based instructional strategies in his teaching (see Fisher & Frey, 2004). It is important to note that Abdurashid scored well enough on the AP Physics exam to receive college credit for the experience.

Now imagine that Abdurashid goes to his next class, and this type of teaching and learning is not available. In that case, he is unlikely to perform as well. For many students, quality content literacy instruction is dependent on the teacher; some provide this type of instruction and some do not. In other schools, different teachers require students to use different content literacy strategies. Imagine how much mental energy Abdurashid would expend if every one of his teachers asked students to use a different note-taking system. Imagine how much easier it would be if all of his teachers agreed on a core set of instructional strategies in the content areas and used those strategies across the day. Abdurashid would spend very little time focused on the strategy and a great deal of time focused on the content. Again, this is what we mean by *transportable* and *transparent*. Let's now turn our attention to a school in which teachers agreed to and delivered specific instructional strategies throughout the day.

## How One Urban School Made a Difference

By all accounts, Herbert Hoover High School in San Diego, California, was a school in trouble (see Fisher, Frey, & Williams, 2002, from which this account is adapted). Achievement scores were the lowest in the county and among the lowest in the state. Teacher morale was low; turnover was high. Crime, poverty, and basic skills were the most frequent topics of conversation on campus. At one point, a consultant suggested that the school should not expect more from its 2,200 students: 46 percent of them were English language learners, 100 percent qualified for free or reduced-priced lunch, and 96 percent were members of minority groups.

The school *did* expect more, however. Every teacher at the school had been working hard to meet students' needs. The school had a health clinic, counselors, and a great library—but the students were not achieving. Then, in 1999, Hoover formed a staff development committee of teachers, administrators, and colleagues from San Diego State University. Together they identified seven instructional strategies that would permeate the school at every level. They wanted the strategies to be transparent to the students, and they wanted literacy strategies in content area instruction to become commonplace—across English, science, social studies, art, physical education, music, and shop. After the school's governance committee approved these strategies, it was expected that every teacher in the school would use them.

Equally important as the commitment *from* teachers was the school's commitment *to* them. This school had seen many reform efforts come and go, and staff members were exhausted from shifting priorities. Hoover needed an unswerving focus. Over the next three years, the professional development committee worked on a professional development plan that centered on the school's adopted strategies, and the results seemed to support the efforts.

Hoover's Gates-MacGinitie scores, for example, which the school used to measure reading achievement, increased from an average 5.9 grade-level equivalent to an average 8.2 grade-level equivalent. Although these scores reminded staff members that student achievement at Hoover still had room for growth, they were encouraged that the average student was reading more than two grade levels higher than had been the case three years earlier. In addition, Hoover met its state accountability targets for the first time in a decade. California uses its official accountability score, the Academic Performance Index, to encourage improved school performance by setting an accountability target for each school based on its assessment results. In 1999–2000, with a baseline score of 444 and a target of 462, Hoover achieved a score of 469. On another measure of reading scores, the Stanford 9, Hoover's 9th graders exceeded district growth between 1998 and 2001; the district's scores increased by 1.5 percent and Hoover's by 2.5 percent. In other words, the students were catching up, and the gap was closing.

## Reading and Writing Increasingly Complex Text

| AREA 2: CONTENT AREA CLASSES<br>2. Do all courses throughout a student's day capitalize on the student's literacy and language as a way to learn new information? | | | | | |
|---|---|---|---|---|---|
| | **5** | **4** | **3** | **2** | **1** |
| **2.3. Students are taught strategies for reading and writing increasingly complex text.** | Strategy instruction is recursive to the point of becoming transparent; students use reading comprehension and writing strategies throughout the school day and year. | | Reading and writing strategies are presented to students, and students are expected to use them on their own. | | No support is provided for reading, and students are expected to respond to end-of-chapter questions. |

The link between strategic teaching and student learning has been the keystone of Hoover's professional development plan. Teachers need ongoing professional development that allows for growth in expertise across departments and with years of teaching experience. All staff members need to study each strategy, practice it in their classrooms with peer support, and eventually assume the responsibility for delivering future staff development.

After reviewing research evidence on the efficacy of the strategies, teachers at Hoover quickly adopted the phrase "seven defensible strategies" as part of the high school's lexicon. The specific instructional strategies the staff selected were anticipatory activities, read-alouds (or shared reading), graphic organizers, vocabulary instruction, writing to learn, structured note taking, and reciprocal teaching (Fisher, 2001a). Teachers attended monthly preparatory meetings to read research reviews of the strategies, discuss the successes and challenges of implementing the approach, and show videotapes of their classes to model the strategies for their peers. The staff development committee also created posters of the seven strategies for display in the classroom so that teachers could refer to them during instruction and students could become familiar with the names of the strategies and their use.

## Anticipatory Activities

Teachers may use a number of ways to engage students in learning, including anticipation guides, quickwrites, discovery activities, and essential questions. Regardless of the type of approach, the goal is to activate students' background and prior knowledge, capture their attention and interest, and demonstrate connections between school and the rest of the world. Robert Marzano's book *Building Background Knowledge for Academic Achievement: Research on What Works in Schools* (2004) provides a wealth of information on this topic.

Anticipation guides like the one that Abdurashid did as part of his physics class activate students' thinking and provide them with an overview of the learning to come (Head & Readence, 1986). Anticipation guides are relatively easy to create. They typically involve three to five statements that are true/false or agree/disagree in nature. Students are provided with space to record their thinking both before and after the instruction. Anticipation guides can be used before an assigned reading, a lecture, or a film, or at any other time that new information is being presented. An anticipation guide for a unit of study on Georgia O'Keeffe might look like the one in Figure 2.3.

Quickwrites are writing prompts that focus students on the topic at hand. As such, they are a useful anticipatory activity. Interesting writing prompts are available at http://www.writersdigest.com/writingprompts.asp. Each of the following writing prompts, used to start a class, ensures that students are focused on the content they are about to learn:

- What does Islam have to do with libraries? (7th grade social studies)
- Hydrogen is the most plentiful element on earth. Why do you think this is the case? (high school biology)
- Describe an algebraic technique for adding and subtracting positive and negative numbers. (9th grade algebra)
- Write a rhyming poem about spring. (middle school language arts)
- Some say that "art is life." Are they right? What do they mean? (high school fine art class)

Another anticipatory activity, a K-W-L (Know, Want, Learn), has become a common way to engage students at Hoover. K-W-L charts (Ogle, 1986) are a great way to hook students into learning. These language charts start with the question "What do you know about the topic?" Following this discussion, students are asked, "What do you still want to know about the topic?"

---

### FIGURE 2.3
### Anticipation Guide for Unit of Study on Georgia O'Keeffe

| Before Lecture<br>A = Agree<br>D = Disagree | Statement | After Lecture<br>A = Agree<br>D = Disagree |
|---|---|---|
|  | Georgia O'Keeffe is known for her work in cubism. |  |
|  | Georgia O'Keeffe painted flowers and desert scenery. |  |
|  | Georgia O'Keeffe was a 20th-century European artist. |  |

Once the unit of study has been completed, the language charts are used again, and students answer the third question, "What did you learn about the topic?"

As a way to open her unit of study on the book *Seedfolks* (Fleischman, 1997), an English teacher first asked her students what they knew about community gardens. Their responses included, "My grandma has one with lots of flowers," "We use them to grow vegetables," and "Poor people can grow something to eat."

Their responses to what they wanted to know included such questions as "Why do people like them?" "What can you grow in San Diego?" "How much land do you need?" and "Are community gardens legal?"

When the students finished the book, visited a community garden, and tried to grow their own plants, the teacher returned to the language chart and asked them, "What did you learn?" Their responses included such comments as "It's not about growing food; it's about having space," "Gardening helps you relax," "The garden was a place for people to meet and talk," "This writer's cool; he knows how to tell a story," and "Growing food is really hard." Like many other teachers, this classroom teacher reports that using K-W-L charts helps students organize their inquiries.

## Read-Alouds and Shared Readings

A read-aloud—or shared reading, a similar activity—is one of the most effective ways for young adults to hear fluent reading (Allen, 2000). The Hoover literacy plan advises that teachers read to their students every day in every class for at least 5 of the 90 minutes. Some teachers read the text aloud while students listen; other teachers read the text aloud while students read along. Most often, the selections are not from the textbook; instead, teachers select other materials that build students' background knowledge, provide them with interesting vocabulary words, and ensure they are hearing fluent reading (Ivey, 2003).

One great source of read-aloud material is picture books. Although many picture books are inappropriate for adolescent audiences, a growing number of them align with the content standards across disciplines. For example, an art teacher read aloud the picture book *My Name Is Georgia* (Winter, 1998) before displaying some of Georgia O'Keeffe's work. Nearby, a U.S. history teacher used an overhead projection to share a newspaper dated September 1, 1939, announcing Germany's invasion of Poland. Both teachers noted that these literacy experiences built and extended background knowledge and vocabulary. Figure 2.4 contains representative examples of picture books used in secondary school classrooms.

Fisher, Flood, Lapp, and Frey (2004) examined the characteristics of quality interactive read-alouds. Their data suggest that expert teachers use the following seven components during their read-alouds:

- The book chosen is appropriate to students' interests and matched to their developmental, emotional, and social levels.
- The selection has been previewed and practiced by the teacher.
- A clear purpose for the read-aloud is established.
- Teachers model fluent oral reading when they read the text.
- The teacher is animated and uses expression.
- Teachers stop periodically and thoughtfully question the students to focus them on specifics of the text.
- Connections are made to independent reading and writing.

Remember that the purpose of the read-aloud is to develop vocabulary, build background knowledge, and foster a love of reading. During a read-aloud, the teacher is the only one who can see the text. This contrasts with a shared reading, in which the students and the teacher can all see the text. Remember that during both read-alouds and shared readings, the *teacher* is the reader.

Although shared readings develop vocabulary, build background knowledge, and foster a love of reading, they are also used to teach a specific feature of the text (Allen, 2000). Instruction in text features could focus on cause-and-effect structures, the use of references in a research paper, how to use a reading strategy such as predictions or questioning, or a host of other concepts.

Let's listen in on a physics class while Ms. Grant conducts a shared-reading lesson. The students are studying force and the causes and effects of force. Ms. Grant has a collection of eggs on her lab table. She picks up an egg and says, "Cause." As she cracks it open on the side of a bowl, she says, "Effect." She picks up another egg and says, "Tina, catch . . . cause." Tina catches the egg and Ms. Grant says, "Effect." Ms. Grant then says, "Anthony, catch . . . cause." Anthony misses the egg, it breaks on the floor, and Ms. Grant says, "Effect." The surprise is evident in the room because the egg has been hardboiled and does not splatter all over the floor. Marita asks Ms. Grant how she knew which egg to toss.

---

**FIGURE 2.4**
**Examples of Picture Books for Older Readers**

### Science

Lee, M. (2001). *Earthquake.* New York: Farrar, Straus, and Giroux.
Scieszka, J., & Smith, L. (2004). *Science verse.* New York: Viking.
Sis, P. (1996). *Starry messenger: Galileo Galilei.* New York: Farrar, Straus, and Giroux.
Sis, P. (2003). *The tree of life: Charles Darwin.* New York: Farrar, Straus, and Giroux.

### Social Studies

Haskins, J., & Benson, K. (1999). *Bound for America: The forced migration of Africans to the new world.*
　　New York: Lothrop, Lee, & Shepard Books.
Krull, K. (2000). *Lives of extraordinary women: Rulers, rebels (and what the neighbors thought).*
　　San Diego, CA: Harcourt.
Palacco, P. (2000). *The butterfly.* New York: Philomel Books.
Tsuchiya, Y. (1951). *Faithful elephants: A true story of animals, people, and war.* Boston:
　　Houghton Mifflin.

### Math

Neuschwander, C. (1997). *Sir Cumference and the first round table.* Watertown, MA: Charlesbridge.
Pappas, T. (1991). *Math talk: Mathematical ideas in poems for two voices.* San Carlos, CA: Wide
　　World Publishing.
Scieszka, J., & Smith, L. (1995). *Math curse.* New York: Viking.
Tang, G. (2001). *The grapes of math.* New York: Scholastic.

### Visual and Performing Arts

Krull, K. (2003). *M is for music.* San Diego, CA: Harcourt.
Ryan, P. M. (2002). *When Marian sang: The true recital of Marian Anderson: The voice of the century.*
　　New York: Scholastic.
Waldman, N. (1999). *The starry night.* Honesdale, PA: Boyds Mills Press.
Weitzman, J. P., & Glasser, R. P. (1998). *You can't take a balloon into the Metropolitan
　　Museum.* New York: Dial Books for Young Readers.

### Exercise and Nutritional Science, Health, and Physical Education

Krull, K. (1997). *Lives of the athletes: Thrills, spills (and what the neighbors thought).* San Diego, CA:
　　Harcourt.
Krull, K. (2000). *Wilma unlimited: How Wilma Rudolph became the world's fastest woman.* New York:
　　Voyager Books.
Taylor, C. (1992). *The house that crack built.* San Francisco: Chronicle Books.
Thomas, K. (2003). *Blades, boards and scooters.* Toronto, Ontario: Maple Tree Press.

Ms. Grant explains that putting an egg on a flat tabletop and spinning it is a way to tell if an egg is raw or hardboiled. A hardboiled egg spins freely, as you would expect, but a raw egg slows down quickly and moves sluggishly, because of the motion of the liquid inside. Now that she has their full attention (as a result of her anticipatory activities), she is ready to begin her shared reading.

Ms. Grant introduces her shared reading—a short explanation of force from the Web site http://physicsweb.org. She has selected "The Physics of Football" from the Web site, which she projects from her computer and data projector. After explaining that "football" means soccer in the United Kingdom, she reads the text aloud, pausing periodically to point out the cause-and-effect statements being made. At one point, the text reads as follows:

> Consider a ball that is spinning about an axis perpendicular to the flow of air across it. The air travels faster relative to the center of the ball where the periphery of the ball is moving in the same direction as the airflow. This reduces the pressure, according to Bernoulli's principle. The opposite effect happens on the other side of the ball, where the air travels slower relative to the center of the ball. There is therefore an imbalance in the forces and the ball deflects—or, as Sir J. J. Thomson put it in 1910, "the ball follows its nose." This lateral deflection of a ball in flight is generally known as the "Magnus effect."

At several places throughout the text, Ms. Grant stops and discusses causes and effects in understanding force. She reminds her students of their previous study of Bernoulli's principle and explains the causes and effects that are understood as the Magnus effect. Although she could have done this as a read-aloud, Ms. Grant wanted her students to read the text with her to gain practice in determining cause and effect—the focus of her lesson.

## Graphic Organizers

Graphic organizers provide students with visual information that complements the class discussion or text. Organizers come in many forms, from Venn diagrams to complex cause-and-effect charts (see Wood, Lapp, & Flood, 1992). Students at Hoover consistently report that the graphic organizer is the most helpful strategy that teachers use. This is consistent with the research on graphic organizers (see, for example, Alvermann, 1991; Robinson, 1998). Enchanted Learning (www.enchantedlearning.com/graphicorganizers/) provides graphic organizers that can be printed directly from the Web site.

Although graphic organizers come in hundreds of versions, they can be organized into four main types: concept maps, flow diagrams, tree diagrams, and matrices (Robinson, 1998).

**Concept Maps.** Concept maps are a series of words organized by their relationship around a central idea. For example, Larry Caudillo, a biology teacher, placed on the board at random a number of magnetic strips with terms on them related to the concept of matter. He invited students to come to the board to create a graphic representation of the information they had been studying (see Figure 2.5 for a sample of student work). He also asked that they draw lines and write in the relationships between the words. One student moved the word *neutron* under the word *nucleus* and wrote "contains" between them. She understood that the nucleus contains neutrons. The next student drew a circle around the words *nucleus, neutron,* and *contains.* He then added the word *electron* to the outside of the circle and wrote "spins in the shell." The science teacher was pleased to see evidence of the students' understanding of this atomic unit's orbital behavior evidenced in the creation of the graphic organizer.

**Flow Diagrams.** These diagrams are used to visually display a process, a sequence of events, or a time line. A simple version of this occurs when students construct time lines as they read their history books. For example, a time line for the U.S. involvement in World War II might look like the one in Figure 2.6. A flow diagram for solving a quadratic equation appears in Figure 2.7.

**Tree Diagrams.** These graphic organizers are often used to classify and categorize information by visually demonstrating how items are related. The tree's "trunk" represents the main topic. The "branches" represent the facts, factors, influences, traits, people, or outcomes that are associated with the main topic. Tree diagrams are especially helpful as students attempt to solve math and science word problems. For example, a textbook might ask the following question on genetics:

> Many types of color blindness are what are called X-linked; that is, determined by genes on the X chromosome. In this case, a woman is carrying one X chromosome with the gene for a particular type of color blindness; her other X chromosome does not have this gene. If she is married to a man who does not have this gene on his X chromosome, consider the following:
>
> • What is the probability that her first child will carry the X chromosome with the gene associated with color blindness?
> • Suppose amniocentesis reveals that the child is male. What is the probability that the child is color-blind?

The tree diagram in Figure 2.8 provides the answers to these questions.

# FIGURE 2.5
## Student Graphic Organizer

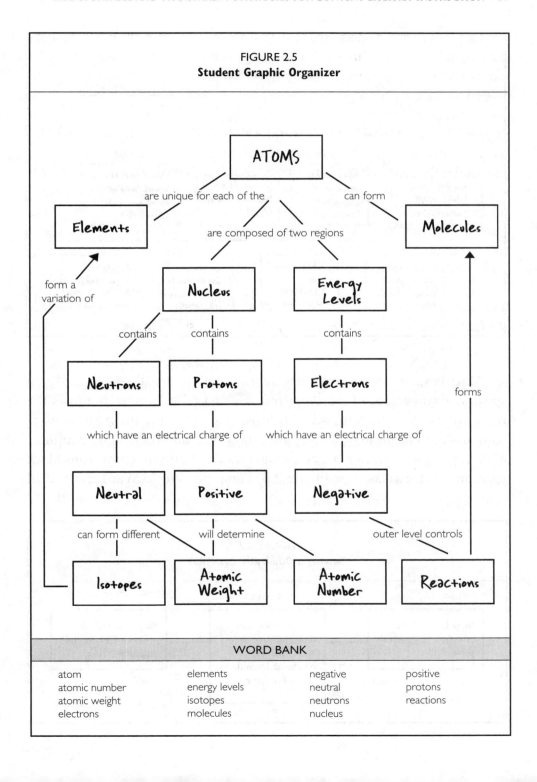

WORD BANK

| | | | |
|---|---|---|---|
| atom | elements | negative | positive |
| atomic number | energy levels | neutral | protons |
| atomic weight | isotopes | neutrons | reactions |
| electrons | molecules | nucleus | |

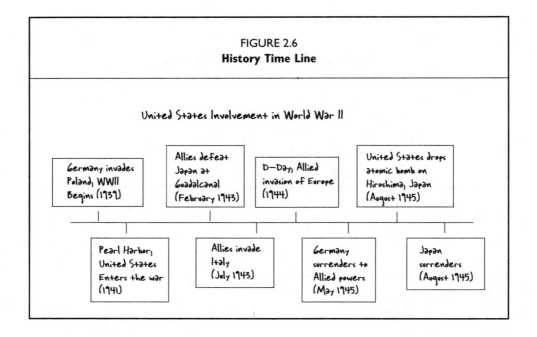

FIGURE 2.6
**History Time Line**

United States Involvement in World War II

Germany invades Poland, WWII Begins (1939)

Allies defeat Japan at Guadalcanal (February 1943)

D—Day, Allied invasion of Europe (1944)

United States drops atomic bomb on Hiroshima, Japan (August 1945)

Pearl Harbor, United States Enters the war (1941)

Allies invade Italy (July 1943)

Germany surrenders to Allied powers (May 1945)

Japan surrenders (August 1945)

**Matrices.** Another way to display information visually is the matrix, a specific arrangement of words or phrases in a table format. It allows the reader to easily distinguish relationships. One use of the matrix is to allow students to determine how things are alike and different. At its simplest, a matrix might look like a Venn diagram. The Venn diagram from Mark Jackson's history class (see Figure 2.9) compares World War I and World

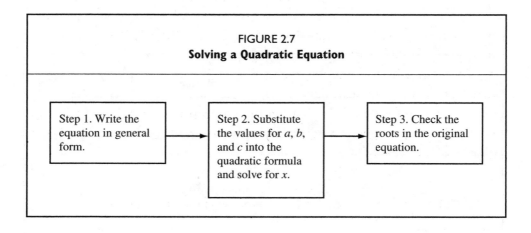

FIGURE 2.7
**Solving a Quadratic Equation**

Step 1. Write the equation in general form.

Step 2. Substitute the values for $a$, $b$, and $c$ into the quadratic formula and solve for $x$.

Step 3. Check the roots in the original equation.

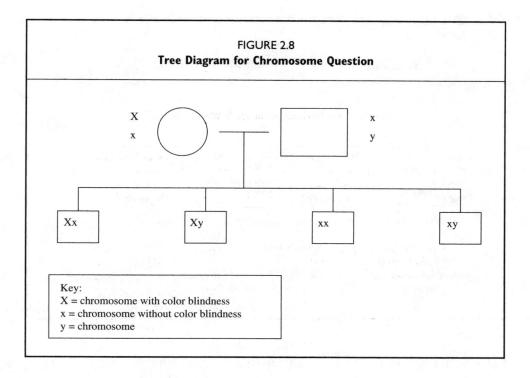

FIGURE 2.8
**Tree Diagram for Chromosome Question**

Key:
X = chromosome with color blindness
x = chromosome without color blindness
y = chromosome

War II. A more complex matrix, like the one in Figure 2.10, provides a more complex comparison of several related items (in this case, classification of the animal kingdom).

## Vocabulary Instruction

Like most middle and high schools, Hoover had student achievement data that consistently reported low scores in vocabulary. It seemed that every teacher focused on different words and used different approaches for teaching vocabulary. Many considered vocabulary knowledge to be the domain of English or elementary school teachers and did not spend much instructional time on vocabulary.

The review of research by Baumann, Kaméenui, and Ash (2003) suggests that a comprehensive vocabulary curriculum have at least the following three objectives:

Objective 1: Teach students to learn words independently.
Objective 2: Teach students the meanings of specific words.
Objective 3: Help students to develop an appreciation for words and to experience enjoyment and satisfaction in their use. (p. 778)

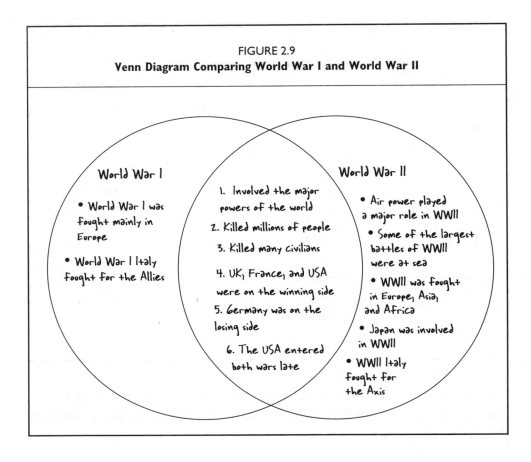

FIGURE 2.9
**Venn Diagram Comparing World War I and World War II**

World War I

- World War I was fought mainly in Europe
- World War I Italy fought for the Allies

1. Involved the major powers of the world
2. Killed millions of people
3. Killed many civilians
4. UK, France, and USA were on the winning side
5. Germany was on the losing side
6. The USA entered both wars late

World War II

- Air power played a major role in WWII
- Some of the largest battles of WWII were at sea
- WWII was fought in Europe, Asia, and Africa
- Japan was involved in WWII
- WWII Italy fought for the Axis

FIGURE 2.10
**Matrix of the Animal Kingdom**

|  | Live Birth | Hair | Vertebrates | Skin or Scales | Cold- or Warm-Blooded |
|---|---|---|---|---|---|
| Reptiles | No | No | Yes | Scales | Cold |
| Amphibians | No | No | Yes | Skin | Cold |
| Birds | No | No | Yes | Skin and feathers | Warm |
| Mammals | Yes | Yes | Yes | Skin | Warm |
| Fish | No | No | Yes | Scales | Cold |

As discussed further in Chapter 3, students can learn words independently (Objective 1) in a number of ways, including independent reading and sustained silent reading. In addition, listening to read-alouds and shared readings, listening to books on tape, and engaging students in classroom discussions and written composition facilitate independent learning of words.

Helping students develop an appreciation for words, Objective 3, is also something that can happen routinely in the secondary school. First, every teacher in the school needs to be a positive role model, demonstrating for students how words can be interesting and how learning words can be fun. In addition, teachers can "play" with words and ensure that students routinely use the vocabulary they have learned at school out of school.

So that leaves Objective 2—the specific words students need to learn. The vocabulary demands on children increase dramatically during the school years, reaching an estimated 88,500 word families by the time a student is in high school (Nagy & Anderson, 1984). Word families are groups of words that have a common root or pattern, such as *judge, adjudicate,* and *judgment.* Given the number of word families, it is estimated that students are exposed to more than 500,000 words while they are in grades 3 through 9. As we have noted, they will learn a number of these words independently. The question, then, is this: Which words do students need specific instruction on?

Vacca and Vacca (2001) suggest that there are three types of vocabulary to consider when selecting words: general, specialized, and technical. *General vocabulary* includes words used in everyday language, usually with widely agreed-upon meanings. These words rarely require specific instruction, but individual students may need help with the definitions of these words.

*Specialized vocabulary* includes words that have multiple meanings in different content areas. For example, in math the word *set* is much more specific than *setting* a table, to *set* your mind on a problem, or to *set* a wedding date.

Finally, *technical vocabulary* words are specific to a field of study. *House of Representatives* in social studies, *photosynthesis* in science, and *rhombus* in mathematics are examples of technical vocabulary because they have a specific meaning associated with a content area.

But the question remains: Which words should be the focus of specific vocabulary instruction? Figure 2.11 contains questions and considerations for selecting vocabulary words. Let's explore each of these as you consider which vocabulary words require specific instruction.

**Representativeness.** Is the potential word representative of an important concept that is necessary for understanding the content or text? Some words are *concepts,* whereas others are *labels.* Given the volume of vocabulary words students must use and master each year, it seems reasonable to suggest that instructional time should focus on concepts and not so much on words that function only as labels in a particular reading. Imagine, for example, reading *The Head Bone's Connected to the Neck Bone: The Weird, Wacky, and Wonderful X-Ray* (McClafferty, 2001). In the first chapter, students will encounter a number of unfamiliar words, including *cathode, contraption, electricity,* and *barium.* Most of these are label words, but electricity

---

### FIGURE 2.11
### Selecting Vocabulary Words

| Considerations for Selecting Vocabulary to Teach | Questions to Ask |
| --- | --- |
| Representativeness | Is the concept represented by the word critical to understanding the lesson, activity, or text? |
| Repeatability | Will the word be used again during the school year in this class? |
| Transportability | Will the word be used in other subject areas or classes? |
| Contextual Analysis | Can students use context clues to determine meaning? |
| Structural Analysis | Can students use structural analysis to determine meaning? |
| Cognitive Load | Have I identified too many words? |

*Source:* From *Language Arts Workshop: Purposeful Reading and Writing Instruction* (p. 275) by N. Frey and D. Fisher, 2007. Upper Saddle River, NJ: Merrill/Prentice Hall. Copyright 2007 by Merrill/Prentice Hall. Adapted with permission.

is a concept that is critical to the understanding of this chapter and thus worth teaching specifically.

**Repeatability.** Is the word going to be used throughout the school year? Some words are worth teaching because they are useful and will be used often. For example, it is worthwhile to provide instruction on the word *rights* in a government class because the term is used regularly and with specific meanings.

**Transportability.** Some words should be selected because they will appear in many subjects or content areas. Teaching students the word *migrant* as it appears in *The Circuit* (Jiménez, 1997) is useful because students will also be using this word in social studies. Similarly, selecting words from specific word families or words that have transportable prefixes, suffixes, and roots can help students understand words that they have not directly been taught.

**Contextual Analysis.** If students can use context clues to determine the word meaning, then direct instruction is not necessary. In reading *Meltdown: A Race Against Nuclear Disaster at Three Mile Island* (Hampton, 2001, p. 3), students can use context clues to determine the meaning of *explosion* based on the way the author uses it in several sentences, including "erupt out of the desert in a blinding flash of light and form into a mushroom-shaped cloud."

**Structural Analysis.** Words that contain affixes and Latin or Greek root words that students are familiar with can be analyzed through structural analysis. For example, the word *justification* may not need to be included in the list of vocabulary words to be taught if students understand the meaning of *justify* and recognize that the suffix -*tion* is used to change verbs into nouns.

**Cognitive Load.** Although educators debate about the number of vocabulary words that should be introduced to students at a given time, most agree that the number should reflect the developmental level of the students and the length of the reading. Most teachers agree that no more than 10 unfamiliar words should be introduced at any one time.

We support the recommendations made by Stahl (1998) that teachers should balance between understanding that students will learn words in context and addressing students' need for systematic, explicit instruction of words. We know that students will learn a great number of words from well-chosen texts *and* from the selection of words for specific instruction.

Now that you have your words selected, what do you do with them? Some of the instructional strategies we see used most often in content area classrooms include concept ladders, vocabulary journals, and word sorts (Blachowicz & Fisher, 2002; Brassell & Flood, 2004).

**Concept Ladders.** Concept ladders are used when selected vocabulary words represent a concept that has many other associated ideas and words. Using concept ladders, students associate words with one another around a central idea. When the target word is identified, students are guided in developing their understanding of the concept by "climbing up the ladder" to identify these attributes:

- What is it a kind of?
- What is it a part of?
- What is it a stage of?
- What is it a product or result of? (Brassell & Flood, 2004, p. 12)

They then "climb down" the ladder to develop examples of the focus word:

- What are kinds of it?
- What are parts of it?
- What are stages of it?
- What are products or results of it? (Brassell & Flood, 2004, p. 12)

A concept ladder for the focus term *Great Depression* appears in Figure 2.12.

**Vocabulary Journals.** Vocabulary journals are a helpful way for students to catalog the words they are learning. For example, the algebra teacher wanted his students to understand that the vocabulary words that he selected had both general and math-specific definitions. He asked students to fill out four columns in special vocabulary journals. In the first column, students wrote a list of words, including *variable, equation,* and *binomial.* Then the students wrote the common definitions of each term in the second column and the math-specific definition in the third column. In the final column, students identified where they had found the accepted math definition; some cited a page in the algebra textbook, while others noted a Web site address or a poster on the bulletin board.

**Word Sorts.** Word sorts require that students use or create categories and then align a series of words in those categories. Word sorts can either be closed (the teacher provides the categories) or open (students create their

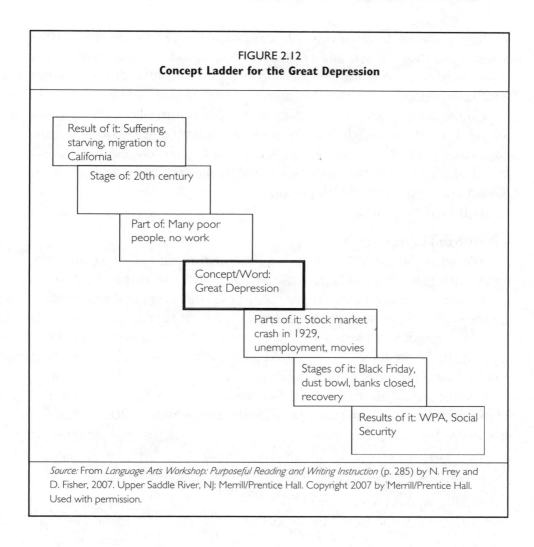

**FIGURE 2.12**
**Concept Ladder for the Great Depression**

Result of it: Suffering, starving, migration to California

Stage of: 20th century

Part of: Many poor people, no work

Concept/Word: Great Depression

Parts of it: Stock market crash in 1929, unemployment, movies

Stages of it: Black Friday, dust bowl, banks closed, recovery

Results of it: WPA, Social Security

*Source:* From *Language Arts Workshop: Purposeful Reading and Writing Instruction* (p. 285) by N. Frey and D. Fisher, 2007. Upper Saddle River, NJ: Merrill/Prentice Hall. Copyright 2007 by Merrill/Prentice Hall. Used with permission.

own categories). Because students rarely produce identical word sorts, especially using open sorts, conversations about their understandings of word meanings occur naturally.

For example, students may be given the following words as a review of their social studies knowledge and be asked to sort them into categories: King, Pearl Harbor, Black Thursday, Roosevelt, Hitler, Discrimination, *Brown v. Board of Education,* concentration camp, Twenty-Fourth Amendment, Wall Street, Churchill, bank run, dust bowl, bread lines, Hiroshima, and Hoovervilles. As students sort the words into categories, they will have to think about the terms and what they mean in relation to other words. Thus word sorts provide students with an opportunity to think about vocabulary and allow the teacher to assess student understanding.

Having said this, it is important to remember the advice of a physics teacher from Hoover High School. As Vince Andrews noted, "Most students have the idea in their head, they just don't know the word for it." He has found that demonstrating an idea, talking about the idea, and then giving students the words for the idea is much more effective than trying to teach vocabulary out of context.

## Writing to Learn

We agree with Fearn and Farnan (2001) that reading, writing, and content learning are related. Teachers use writing-to-learn strategies at the beginning, middle, or end of class to help students inquire about, clarify, or reflect on the content. The student thinks for a minute or so, and then writes for about five minutes. Some teachers begin class with this strategy to help students focus on the topic. Students told us that it was difficult to think about a social conversation that they had had earlier in the day when they were actively writing about the stock market crash. Other teachers conclude their classes by asking for a summary of what students learned in class, a description of one highlight of the class, or a prediction of what the class would study the next day. Regardless of how teachers implement this strategy, writing helps students think about the content, reflect on their knowledge of the content, and share their thoughts with the teacher.

Let's consider an example from a middle school math class working on inequality problems. Students in this class were asked to select one of the problems they had solved as part of the homework and to write an explanation of how they solved the problem. Alberto selected his problem and wrote the following:

> I learn how to do inequality problems in Mr. Uhuru's class. First I thought it was hard, but now it is easy. It is easy because I come after school to get help.

Miguel selected his problem and wrote this:

> I learned how to solve inequalities just by pretending the symbol $(<, >)$ is an equal sign $(=)$, so then I can solve it like I solve problems to find the unknown. I also learned that if I divide or multiply both sides by a negative number, I have to change the symbol. For example, if the symbol was $\geq$, I would change it to $\leq$. I learned how to graph

inequalities as well. I learned that if the symbol has a line under it ($\geq$), I should shade in the circle when I graph it. If there isn't a line under it ($<$), it means that $x$ or the variable isn't equal, so I should leave the circle unshaded.

Although both students got their problem sets correct, their writing provided the teacher with information about what students understood and what they still needed to learn.

Fisher and Frey (2004, pp. 142–143) identified a number of writing-to-learn prompts that can be used across content areas, including the following:

• *Admit Slips.* Upon entering the classroom, students write on an assigned topic such as, "What did you notice was important in yesterday's discussion?" or "Explain the difference between jazz and rock."

• *Crystal Ball.* Students describe what they think class will be about, what will happen next in the novel they are reading, or the next step in a lab experiment.

• *Found Poems.* Students reread an assigned text and find key phrases that "speak" to them, then arrange these into a poem structure without adding any of their own words.

• *Awards.* Students recommend someone or something for an award that the teacher has created, such as "the best artist of the century, living or dead."

• *Cinquains.* Students write a five-line poem in which the first line is the topic (a noun), the second line is a description of the topic in two words, the third line is three "ing" words, the fourth line is a description of the topic in four words, and the final line is a synonym of the topic word from line one.

• *Yesterday's News.* Students summarize the information presented the day before, either from a film, lecture, discussion, or reading.

• *"What If" Scenarios.* Students respond to prompts in which information is changed from what they know, and they predict outcomes. For example, students may be asked to respond to, "What would be different if the Civil War had been fought in 1920?"

• *Take a Stand.* Students discuss their opinions about a controversial topic such as, "Just because we can, should we clone people?"

• *Letters.* Students write letters to others, including elected officials, family members, friends, or people who made a difference. For example, students may respond to the prompt, "Write a letter to Dr. Martin Luther King Jr. informing him of the progress we have made on racism since his death."

• *Exit Slips.* As a closure activity, students write on an assigned prompt such as, "The three best things I learned today are. . ."

## Note Taking

The ability to take and organize notes is a significant predictor of student success. Notes serve an external storage function that builds comprehension and understanding of the content. Over time, and with instruction, students use their notes not only for external storage of information but also for encoding their ideas. In a review of note-taking instruction, Ganske (1981) suggests that note taking is a critical skill that must be fostered. Similarly, Pauk (2001) observed that note taking was a critical skill for success in college. Further, Peverly, Brobst, Graham, and Shaw (2003) showed that background knowledge and note taking were significant predictors of success on tests.

In other words, note taking is a critical skill. But the question remains, what kind of note-taking system works? According to a number of studies, a two-column format such as Cornell note taking is effective (see, for example, Fisher, 2001b; Spires & Stone, 1989). Using this format (which we described earlier in the account of Abdurashid), students take notes and complete the tasks on the right side of the page, while using the left side for main ideas and key words (see Figure 2.2). These main ideas and key words help students quickly find information, locate references, and study for exams. As Faber, Morris, and Lieberman (2000) found, the Cornell note-taking system increases comprehension and test scores. Teaching students to use the system is not difficult. The key is to have a system that everyone at the school agrees to use.

Teachers at Hoover quickly noticed the effects of the implementation of this strategy because they realized that they no longer had to devote instructional time to teaching a study technique. They were then able to turn their instructional focus from the *process* of note taking to the *products* of note taking. Considering the products of note taking requires that teachers regularly collect student notes and give students feedback.

## Reciprocal Teaching

Reciprocal teaching (Carter, 1997; Oczkus, 2003; Palincsar & Brown, 1984) allows students to become the instructors of the content that they are studying. Working in groups of four, students read a text passage together, following a protocol for predicting, questioning, clarifying, and summarizing—

skills that teachers have modeled over a series of lessons until students are comfortable assuming these assigned roles. These student-directed discussion groups can then monitor their comprehension and reinforce their understanding.

In a physical education class, for example, the teacher introduced the rules of volleyball by providing students with a text that explained all the rules of the game. He could have explained the rules verbally, but he knew that reading, asking questions, and clarifying the rules in small groups would both foster literacy skills and increase his students' understanding of the game. When a group of students were overheard remarking, "Hey, isn't this reciprocal teaching?" it was obvious that the faculty at this school had succeeded in making this strategy transportable and transparent.

## Selecting Texts in Content Classes

**AREA 2: CONTENT AREA CLASSES**

*2. Do all courses throughout a student's day capitalize on the student's literacy and language as a way to learn new information?*

| | 5 | 4 | 3 | 2 | 1 |
|---|---|---|---|---|---|
| **2.4. Selected texts span a range of difficulty levels.** | Students learn important concepts through reading a range of texts including informational sources, short stories, biographies, poems, diaries, journals, primary sources, graphic novels, picture books, songs, and electronic sources. | | Textbooks are supplemented with whole-class readings such as a newspaper or magazine article. | | Grade-level textbooks are used. |

Think back to when you were reading content area information in middle school, high school, college, or even graduate school. Does the grade-level, subject-specific textbook bring back warm memories for you? Perhaps you were one of the rare students who read assignments enthusiastically, even reading ahead because you were so intrigued. Or maybe you were one of the many students who read dutifully as chapters were assigned, but what went through your head as you were reading was something akin to, "How much more do I have left?" or "Whew! Finally finished!" without really taking in the information or remembering what you read. Some of you tried to remember because you had teachers who were famous for giving pop quizzes to check on who had read the assignment. Then there were others of you who simply did not do the reading, either because you could circumvent it and still get an A or because it was just too boring or did not make sense to you.

All the strategy work in the world cannot compensate for texts that are boring or extremely difficult for students to read. As we noted in Chapter 1 and will emphasize again in Chapter 3, students need access to a wide variety of books. This variety should apply in terms of reading difficulty, genres, and topics. In the case of content area classes, students need to read across genres to really develop a strong understanding of the discipline (see, for example, Hynd, 1999).

One way to nearly ensure that students will *not* learn specific information from their reading is to give them books on the topic that are too difficult for them. A good rule of thumb is that if you want students to learn a particular concept, look for reading materials that students can read almost effortlessly or with little support. As a reader, when you do not have to exert all of your mental energy on just figuring out the words or taking in unfamiliar concepts, then you can focus on the learning objectives. How often does this happen for all students in a one-size-fits-all textbook? Rarely, if ever, especially if you teach content to students who still find reading and writing difficult. Plus, who ever became an expert on a topic from reading only the textbook?

We think the gold standard of content area reading materials has been reached by schools such as Thomas Harrison Middle School in Harrisonburg, Virginia. The staff at Harrison developed a literacy library full of materials linked to a range of student learning needs, including those embodied in the Virginia Standards of Learning. We talk more about the literacy library in Chapter 5. Essentially, this is a room housing collections of materials built around the wide range of developmental reading needs in this school and including masses of informational texts for content area teachers to use.

To get an idea of how the literacy library benefits students and teachers in content area classrooms, let's take a look into Mr. Powell's 7th grade history class. As students begin a unit on westward expansion in the United States during the 1800s, Mr. Powell reads aloud from *Liberty for All?*, a volume from Joy Hakim's (2002) *A History of Us* series. Everyone has a copy of the text, but Mr. Powell reads it himself, demonstrating all of the characteristics of high-quality interactive read-alouds that we discussed earlier in this chapter. This text is interesting, but the reading levels in this class, which includes special education students, second-language learners, and students in remedial reading programs, range from around the 2nd grade level all the way through the high school level, making it unreasonable to ask students to read independently. In addition, Mr. Powell reads aloud excerpts from other books as they cover specific topics related to the big theme of westward expansion, such as *The Perilous Journey of the Donner Party* (Calabro, 1999), and *Mountain Men: True Grit and Tall Tales* (Glass, 2001).

After days of providing lots of background information through teacher read-alouds and class discussions, Mr. Powell then asks students to become more expert on one topic each that intrigued them. The literacy library contains dozens and dozens of different titles on topics such as the California gold rush, the Oregon Trail, and the Pony Express. The books available include informational picture books, biographies, books in diary or journal format, and historical fiction; they vary in difficulty levels to match students' reading abilities. (For examples of books chosen by students, see Figure 2.13.) Students work independently or in pairs to read their selected text and then, based on what they learned, write their own text as a way to share their expertise with the rest of the class.

We were particularly interested in Robin, a struggling reader who rarely participated in class activities. She could most often be found resting her head on her desk during class time, completely lethargic and out of touch with what was happening. The opportunity to learn from a book she could actually read is what facilitated Robin's participation in history class. Along with two other students who also struggled to read grade-level materials, she chose *Kit Carson: A Life of Adventure* (Mercati, 2000). As they began to write, we saw Robin engaged as never before in history class. It was clear that she had read and learned as she dictated information for Maria to type on the computer:

- He learned how to speak Spanish, French, and several other languages.
- Kit is short for Christopher.
- In 1842 John C. Fremont hired Kit as a guide. He and his men were to map out the Rocky Mountains.

---

**FIGURE 2.13**
**Examples of Books on Westward Expansion Available in a Literacy Library**

Blashfield, J. F. (2001). *The Santa Fe trail (We the people)*. Minneapolis, MN: Compass Point Books.
Garland, S. (2000). *Voices of the Alamo*. New York: Scholastic.
Harness, C. (1996). *"They're off": The story of the Pony Express*. New York: Simon & Schuster.
Krensky, S. (1996). *Striking it rich: The story of the California gold rush*. New York: Aladdin.
Lavendar, D. (1996). *Snowbound: The tragic story of the Donner party*. New York: Scholastic.
McNeer, M. (1950). *The California gold rush*. New York: Random House.
Thompson, G. (2002). *Our journey west: The Marshall family on the Oregon Trail, 1853*. Washington, DC: National Geographic Society.

---

These girls printed and pasted the information they wrote, filling one entire side of a poster board. Robin suggested that they could use the flip side as well.

Having readable, interesting materials makes it possible for all students to learn from reading. Using one grade-level textbook often ensures that students who struggle will have to rely on just listening to learn the required information. Using diverse materials not only provides students with better access to the information, but also makes the subjects you teach more interesting. We constantly get questions from teachers about how to motivate students to read in the content areas. The simple answer is this: Get better, more readable books.

✱ ✱ ✱ ✱ ✱ ✱ ✱

If your experiences with getting students to read and write in your subject area have been grim, with students either resisting reading or merely complying by reading without engagement and understanding, then ask yourself the question we asked at the beginning of this chapter: Do your courses capitalize on students' literacy and language as a way to learn new information? Chances are, much of students' content reading has only highlighted their difficulty with informational text and made them appear uninterested in learning about school-sanctioned topics. If you set the expectation that students can learn through reading and writing, teach them transparent, transportable strategies, and provide access to books on your subject that are readable and worth reading, you will likely discover student interest in your topic that is otherwise difficult to detect.

# 3

## Time Spent "Just Reading": A Nonnegotiable

> I like that we get to choose our own book. It gives you something to think about, and it's not boring. I don't like how it's such a short time.
> —Keisha, 6th grader

Keisha's sentiments about the value of independent reading in school mirror the perspectives of many secondary students. That is, independent reading is an important part of the school day (Brozo & Hargis, 2003; Fisher, 2004; Ivey & Broaddus, 2001). How seriously do you take the role of "just reading" in school? What level of prominence does time spent actually reading hold in the overall vision for literary development in your district, school, or classroom? Our essential question for this chapter is this:

*Are all students provided with an opportunity to read for learning and pleasure during the school day?*

We argue that reading itself is perhaps the most important contributor to growth in reading ability. However, it is doubtful that most middle and high schools are at a point where students spend a substantial amount of time during the instructional day actually engaged in text. In this chapter we urge you to consider the role that "just reading" plays in reading development and in content learning. First, we explore research on the benefits of time spent reading. Then we look at how one high school resuscitated a schoolwide independent reading time that, like some programs in your experience, had been inconsistently implemented over time. Next we examine the unexpected benefits of sustained reading on content learning in a middle school science classroom. Finally, we offer some practical suggestions for making sure independent, wide reading time counts for all students in the school, and particularly for students who struggle the most to read.

## Why "Just Reading" Is Crucial

Teachers and administrators have been receiving mixed messages about the value of independent silent reading. No doubt you have heard or read about the National Reading Panel's report (2000, pp. 12–13) that concluded that the panel "was unable to find a positive relationship between programs and instruction that encourage large amounts of independent reading and improvements in reading achievement, including fluency." This finding appears, at first glance, to fly in the face of long-standing recommendations that free voluntary reading is the most powerful tool for increasing students' reading abilities (see Dwyer & Reed, 1989; Krashen, 1993). Without a closer examination of the facts, consumers of the National Reading Panel's report might wonder whether all those years of advocating and scheduling for schoolwide reading times, such as sustained silent reading (SSR) and Drop Everything and Read (DEAR), were worthwhile after all.

On the contrary, the evidence base for wide independent reading is as solid as ever. Krashen (2004) points out the insufficiency of the National Reading Panel's claims, which were based on only 14 separate comparisons:

> Of the 14 comparisons, 4 had positive results (students who engaged in free voluntary reading outperformed control groups in traditional language arts classes), and 10 showed no difference between the two groups. In no case did students in sustained silent reading do worse. (p. 20)

Krashen also alerts us to the fact that only specific kinds of studies were included in the panel's review, and a host of other studies revealing the benefits of sustained silent reading, including long-term studies, were excluded (Krashen, 2001).

Blatantly excluded from the review were the correlational studies indicating a strong connection between reading achievement and time spent reading (for a thorough review of correlational, contrastive, and explanatory studies of time spent reading, see Allington, 2001). Even the National Reading Panel admits that "literally hundreds of correlational studies find that the best readers read the most and that poor readers read the least" (p. 12). Good, experienced classroom teachers who have seen struggling readers become more competent at reading through practice would likely agree. Unfortunately, correlational studies did not fit the panel's criteria for selecting studies to review. But can we really afford to ignore this strong evidence base simply because the panel decided it did not suit their purposes? Allington (2001) reminds us that time spent reading remains a research-based, nonnegotiable approach for building reading competence:

> It would seem that the consistency of the evidence surrounding the relationship of volume of reading and reading achievement is surely strong enough to support recommending attention to reading volume as a central feature of the design of any intervention focused on improving reading achievement. (p. 32)

Teachers and administrators in middle and high schools will now find even more research yielding a variety of additional reasons for making "just reading" a priority across the school day. In a survey of 6th graders across 109 classrooms in 23 schools (Ivey & Broaddus, 2001), a majority of the 1,765 students cited independent reading as one of their most preferred activities in language arts class. When asked what they found special about time to read, students consistently said that it allowed them to think and to learn. Later in this chapter we consider students' perspectives on time spent reading as it relates to content learning across the school day, when thinking about and learning specific information and concepts are imperative. Other studies (Stewart, Paradis, Ross, & Lewis, 1996; Worthy & McKool, 1996) indicate that older students, particularly those who struggle with reading, believe that time set aside for reading during the school day makes a difference in their reading improvement and in their inclination to read.

Regardless of how you interpret the research, it is difficult to round up even one real case of a struggling older reader who became a more competent, motivated reader without having spent considerable time engaged in text. What might create barriers for some schools in their attempts to make time spent reading a priority has little to do with the uncertainty about relevant research and more to do with actual implementation and support for it within the school day. We now turn our attention to one school's realization of the importance of independent reading and its efforts to renew and solidify implementation of a schoolwide reading initiative.

## Solidifying the Status of Independent Reading Schoolwide

| AREA 3: SUSTAINED SILENT READING/INDEPENDENT READING<br>3. Are all students provided with an opportunity to read for learning and pleasure during the school day? | | | | | |
|---|---|---|---|---|---|
| | **5** | **4** | **3** | **2** | **1** |
| **3.1. Instructional time is dedicated to self-selected reading.** | Daily instructional time is dedicated to self-selected reading, and school policies and procedures support the use of this time. | | Self-selected reading time is implemented inconsistently or only in selected English classes. | | Students are not provided with an opportunity to read during the school day. |

Teachers may find it difficult to make voluntary free reading time a priority (Worthy, Turner, & Moorman, 1998). Covering the school, district, or state-mandated curriculum often takes precedence over self-selected reading, even in the classrooms of teachers who are convinced by research about the value of reading. This was true even for Herbert Hoover High School, which not only had established a 20-minute schoolwide reading period, but also had implemented a highly successful literacy plan that focused on the specific transportable and transparent strategies we discussed in Chapter 2. In short, this was a school firmly committed to students' literacy development, yet still struggling to maintain its plan to ensure independent reading.

Precipitated by one student's concern that the 20-minute daily reading time was beginning to fall by the wayside as other curricular concerns took precedence, teachers, professional development personnel, and researchers in this school organized an action research project to understand and refurbish sustained silent reading (Fisher, 2004). English department faculty members determined that first it was necessary to get a more accurate picture of what was really happening during sustained silent reading. Observational data on individual students from across 20 randomly selected classrooms during SSR indicated that the student who initially voiced her concern was absolutely right: the SSR time was not consistently used for reading. In many cases, the period was used for extra instruction in the content area, for homework completion, or as free time.

Given the inconsistency of adherence to SSR time, the school's literacy committee decided to examine whether independent reading really made a difference in students' reading achievement. Was this a fight worth fighting? Student scores on the Gates-MacGinitie test from the previous school year helped the committee make that determination. The committee identified eight 9th grade teachers, including four who were consistent in implementing SSR and four who rarely gave students time to read. Although scores from September for the students in these two groups revealed no significant differences, spring scores indicated that students who were provided with time to read independently every day had statistically higher reading scores (.6 of a year, $t = -8.83$, $p < .001$). Imagine what a difference independent reading could make for these students if they made an extra half-year's growth each year over a period of years. Sustained silent reading at Herbert Hoover High School seemed to be well worth salvaging.

The next step was to change teacher attitudes regarding SSR. In addition to setting an "opportunity to read" standard that was to be held in the same regard as content area standards, the principal announced a new task force on SSR. The task force's first charge was to invite student representatives to staff development meetings to offer testimonials about the value of sustained silent reading. After each presentation, teachers were asked to respond in writing to a prompt about what they would do to ensure their students met the "opportunity to read" standard.

Although these presentations and the earlier data collected convinced teachers of the benefits of SSR, doubts lingered about implementation and sustainability. A book by Janice Pilgreen (2000) called *The SSR Handbook* helped SSR task force members to identify some possible sources for the problems as well as some promising solutions. Pilgreen's eight factors for successful implementation of a schoolwide SSR program (see Figure 3.1) helped them to see that simply providing time for reading and creating positive attitudes among teachers and students were not enough. The committee used these eight factors to create a survey for teachers on how well the Hoover SSR program met each of these criteria. Results from the survey indicated that more professional development meetings would need to focus on implementing SSR and in particular on follow-up activities and access to books. In addition, the video production class was brought on board to create commercials for SSR to be shown during staff development sessions and during regular school announcement times.

---

FIGURE 3.1
**Eight Factors of SSR Success**

**1. Access.** This principle deals with getting reading materials into the hands of students, which Pilgreen sees as the responsibility of the teachers and the schools. This involves more than simply telling students they must bring something to read.

**2. Appeal.** This factor deals with student interests, the variety and range of materials we offer to our students, and, yes, even making sure that the materials we offer are "classroom appropriate."

**3. Environment.** This has to do with physical comfort, alternatives to the traditional classroom setting, and the possibilities of reading as a social interactive activity for those students for whom reading in silence is not conducive to the freedom associated with SSR.

**4. Encouragement.** This includes modeling, discussions, and postreading opportunities for sharing, and enlisting parent support and involvement.

**5. Staff training.** Providing training in SSR, answering organizational and "how to" questions, and encouraging all teachers to provide a specific set daily time for SSR are discussed.

**6. Nonaccountability.** While students are not required to complete the usual types of formal assessment, such as book reports or tests of content knowledge, SSR practices do provide for informal accountability through opportunities for sharing in discussion, writing, or other formats.

**7. Follow-up activities.** SSR, Pilgreen says, needs to provide ways for students to "sustain their excitement about the books they have read" (p. 16). Activities and shared experiences are very effective in encouraging further voluntary reading.

**8. Distributed time to read.** Habits—including the habit of reading—are formed through sustained efforts over time. Occasional lengthy periods of time set aside for free reading are not as powerful as shorter periods of 15 to 20 minutes at least twice a week.

*Source:* From "Book review: *The SSR handbook*" by H. M. Miller. (2002). *Journal of Adolescent & Adult Literacy, 45,* pp. 434–435. Copyright 2002 by International Reading Association. Reprinted with permission.

---

## Access to Texts

One particular concern at Hoover was access to readable, interesting books in all classrooms, not just the rooms of the English teachers. Knowing that having just the right materials is what counts most in getting students to read (Ivey & Broaddus, 2001), the school allotted each teacher $800 to purchase books for SSR. After it became apparent on the first round that teachers had purchased mostly narrative texts, a second allotment of $500 per teacher was granted with an understanding that the purchases should reflect a balance between fiction and informational texts. In addition, SSR committee mem-

| AREA 3: SUSTAINED SILENT READING/INDEPENDENT READING | | | | | |
|---|---|---|---|---|---|
| 3. Are all students provided with an opportunity to read for learning and pleasure during the school day? | | | | | |
| | **5** | **4** | **3** | **2** | **1** |
| **3.2. Students have access to diverse texts.** | School and classroom libraries are well stocked with diverse adolescent literature and informational texts; teachers actively seek out books for individual students. | | Teachers' classroom libraries are available but stagnate throughout the year, or students are expected to visit the school library to access books. | | Students read from assigned class readings or are expected to bring their own reading material. |

bers scoured bookstores regularly and solicited donations to acquire materials students preferred to read. A book browsing room was established for teachers to routinely review extra books and new books that they could add to their collections. To help students who still had difficulty getting started and remaining engaged in reading, teachers began to routinely invite key faculty and staff members (such as the assistant principal and the reading specialist) to visit their classrooms and talk about issues such as book selection or attitudes toward reading.

Did all of these efforts lead to more independent reading during SSR? A status check two years into this focused initiative, using the same observational protocol from the exploratory phase of this action research project, indicated that 88 percent of the students were actually reading. Whereas only about 720 students seemed to be engaged during SSR at the onset of the project, roughly 1,940 students appeared to be on board just two years later.

What can other secondary schools take from the lessons learned at Hoover High School? First, students' voices are important barometers for determining what is working and what is needed to build and maintain students' inclination and ability to read. Remember that one student who felt strongly about her own need for sustained reading time during the school day instigated this process. Second, schoolwide initiatives that work require both time and support. Third, and related, the administrator needs to be present in classrooms as the initiatives are taking place and should also maintain a strong, consistent voice in support of the initiative during professional development meetings. Fourth, it makes sense to use actual data to make policy decisions. In the case of this project, information was collected over time and cyclically from students and teachers, from student reading assessments, through observational and survey methods, and from the professional literature. Finally, professional development regarding the implementation of SSR for teachers across the content areas was a key factor in the program's success. Simply allowing time for reading was not sufficient. Teachers need to develop expertise in supporting reading engagement.

Later in this chapter we take an even closer look at what teachers can do to make independent reading time, in all of its forms, count for all students, and in particular the students who seem most resistant and most challenged by reading. But first, we look at the roles and purposes independent reading may play within the official curriculum, with reading attached to actual content standards.

## Beyond SSR: Independently Reading to Learn Science

When Ivey and Broaddus (2001) surveyed 1,765 students in 6th grade, they found that time for independent reading was students' most preferred activity in language arts classes. In addition, students indicated that what made reading time most motivating for them was having accessible, personally interesting books. If time to read and good materials are necessary for reading engagement in language arts classrooms, it stands to reason that these two factors would also be required for purposeful reading in other content area classes. When asked specifically why time for "just reading" was so important, students indicated that this was an important time for deep learning. As one student put it, "I like it because it's quiet and because you get to just think and you don't have to answer questions" (Ivey & Broaddus, 2001, p. 360).

Given students' reasons for silent reading, it seems imperative that we consider how opportunities for extended time with text affect students' attitudes toward reading in the subject areas and their learning of school-sanctioned topics. This was the purpose of one study of independent reading connected to 7th grade life science standards (Ivey & Broaddus, 2003). This investigation took place in Harvey Middle School, a diverse public school serving grades 6 through 8 with a population of just under 1,000 students, located in a small city in a rural area in the southeastern United States. Demographics are constantly changing in this school, which has experienced a recent increase in new students from families who have immigrated to the United States from Spanish-speaking countries and Ukraine.

The focus classroom consisted of 25 students, with 16 students submitting parental consent forms to participate in the study. Three students in the classroom were in an ESL program, and several of the participating students received special education services. Reading levels in this classroom, as reported by the team's language arts teacher and measured using the Qualitative Reading Inventory-3, the Degrees of Reading Power test, and the STAR assessment, ranged from the emergent level through the secondary level. The teacher, Mrs. Nordstrom, was in her second year of teaching, and her subject matter expertise was secondary science. She was interested in learning about science trade books and how they might help her teach required content. Mrs. Nordstrom did not use a textbook for instruction before the study because she questioned its appropriateness in terms of both level of difficulty and interest.

On this particular 7th grade team, SSR was implemented during an extended 5th-period class. Students read materials of their own choosing for the first 20 minutes before beginning the content instruction. In general, students were expected to bring their own texts from home or from the library. Some students used this time to complete assigned reading for their language arts class. With the cooperation of Mrs. Nordstrom, Ivey and Broaddus began introducing to the class trade books related to the 7th grade life science standards they were studying (examples of books related to the theme of animal adaptation, for example, are listed in Figure 3.2). Students were told that they could either continue reading their own books unrelated to science during SSR time, or they could select from the life science trade books. At any given time, 150 to 200 science trade books were available, spanning difficulty levels (emergent to high school level) and formats (including, for example, photographic journals, picture books, diaries, sophisticated informational texts, field journals and scrapbooks, cumulative texts, and novels with embedded science information).

Regardless of what they read, each student kept a daily log, including the title and author of the book, how much the student read, and reasons to recommend or reject each book. Additional data sources included classroom observations, interviews with students and the teacher, ongoing documentation of the materials placed in the classroom, as well as the researchers' and

---

**FIGURE 3.2**
**Examples of Books on Animal Adaptation**

Baker, J. (2000). *The hidden forest.* New York: Greenwillow.
Breidahl, H. (2001). *Extremophiles: Life in extreme environments.* Broomall, PA: Chelsea House.
Dewey, J. O. (2001). *Antarctic journal: Four months at the bottom of the world.* New York: HarperCollins.
Goodman, S. E. (2001). *Claws, coats, and camouflage: The ways animals fit into their world.* Brookfield, CT: Millbrook.
Lewin, T., & Lewin, B. (2000). *Elephant quest.* New York: HarperCollins.
Mallory, K. (2001). *Swimming with hammerhead sharks.* Boston: Houghton Mifflin.
Patent, D. H. (2000). *Slinky scaly slithery snakes.* New York: Walker & Company.
Settel, J. (1999). *Exploding ants: Amazing facts about how animals adapt.* New York: Atheneum.

---

Mrs. Nordstrom's introductions of new science books as they were added to the classroom collection.

Four prominent themes emerged from students' engagement in reading during this time. First, it was not difficult to get students to read about science independently, given time and materials. With the exception of one student who returned to reading fictional novels, everyone opted for science texts over other materials during free reading times. Their decisions to read science were largely driven by a desire to learn. For instance, before the study began, Lee, who was a struggling reader, chose books about football. However, as he began to read science books, he reported that his eyes were open to new information on topics such as animal and plant evolution: "Football is just a sport, and [science books] tell you about history, like snakes and plants and stuff and how they first formed and how they first came to the earth, and how they survive." It is also important to know that during regular whole-class lectures and other activities during science instructional time, Lee was rarely engaged in the subject matter. For students like Lee, independent reading may be one of the best ways to learn the content.

Second, students' book selections were driven by interest. Consistent with the findings of Moss and Hendershot (2002), students' curiosity to know specific information greatly influenced their choices. Students pursued particular topics in their reading and made connections to prior knowledge during one-on-one reading times with the researchers (for example, selecting books about forensic science based on information from the Discovery Channel).

This desire to read for more information was contagious, and students were eager to share what they were learning. Aaron commented on *Tough Beginnings: How Baby Animals Survive* (Singer, 2001), "It's not easy when your dad wants to eat you."

Third, books' difficulty levels were connected to students' choices and persistence with reading. Easy books were overwhelmingly popular across students, whereas students rarely selected highly complex texts. As one struggling reader reported, "Some of the books are hard to read, and I want to be sure that I'm reading the book right . . . the important details." When students understood what they were reading, they persisted. Conversely, when struggling readers chose books that were too difficult, they did not read. Deliberate instruction by the researchers and the teacher was necessary to help some students select books that made sense to them. Lee noted after a frustrating experience with difficult vocabulary in *The Man-Eating Tigers of Sundarbans* (Montgomery, 2001), "It's good to read if you can read it."

Fourth, connections between free-choice reading of life science texts and the official science class were evident, but minimal. As Mrs. Nordstrom became more familiar with life science trade books through her own reading, she began to use some of them during regular science instruction, but mainly as teacher read-alouds. In particular, she was drawn to books that emphasized particular content as she was planning to teach it (for example, plant adaptation). Even though students were largely engaged in reading the science books, reading within the actual instructional time devoted to a specific topic as it was being studied never became a priority. However, students did select some readings about prior topics of study (such as genetics) after listening to book talks that made high-interest connections (e.g. research studies of twins or use of DNA in forensic science). Students did not readily link what they were reading and what they were studying in class unless the teacher used the books for instruction. If middle and secondary content teachers are to make the most of independent reading in their subject area, they should make explicit connections between each unit of study and the books available for free reading.

Although this was just one study in one classroom, it leaves us optimistic and more curious than ever about the benefits of "just reading" in content classrooms. Just as in SSR, though, it was apparent that to make independent reading count for all students, more attention must be paid to what the *teacher* must do to make the time worthwhile for all students. We conclude this chapter with some final words on developing teacher expertise to implement student silent reading times.

## Supporting Inexperienced and Reluctant Readers During Independent Reading

| AREA 3: SUSTAINED SILENT READING/INDEPENDENT READING<br>3. Are all students provided with an opportunity to read for learning and pleasure during the school day? | | | | | |
|---|---|---|---|---|---|
| | **5** | **4** | **3** | **2** | **1** |
| 3.3. Teachers ensure that self-selected reading time matters for students. | Teachers model reading and support students in their self-selected reading by helping them select appropriate texts, helping them get started reading, and helping them overcome dilemmas in their reading. | | Teachers model reading during self-selected reading time. | | Teachers complete other duties or lecture during self-selected reading times. |

Although it is important for teachers to serve as role models by reading on their own during independent reading times and sharing their own reading interests, it will likely be necessary to use this time to get struggling readers started with reading and to help them remain engaged. After all, it is improbable that the most inexperienced readers will take to sustained silent reading without additional support, especially in comparison with the more competent readers who already have the habit of reading voluntarily outside school. Our intention is not to encourage teachers to interrupt the reading of individual students but rather to encourage them to offer instruction and assistance that will allow students to take control of their own reading. We borrow the following three categories of support from Worthy, Broaddus, and Ivey (2001):

*Help students find materials they can read and want to read.* More often than not, this will mean finding relatively easy materials. By the time students reach middle and high school, they are expected to read lengthy and complex chapter books—a challenging requirement for any student who has not yet read any book in its entirety. Teachers can direct students to shorter, more manageable, and interesting texts that allow students to take small but productive steps toward more difficult reading. On the other hand, if students select books that are too hard, they will likely give up on reading, become distracted, or cause other students to be distracted from their reading. For instance, 8th grader and second-language learner José flipped aimlessly through high-interest but too-difficult magazines such as *Sports Illustrated* day after day until his teacher introduced to him some easier texts such as the poem/rap book, *Hey You! C'Mere: A Poetry Slam* (Swados, 2002), which fed his love for rhythmic language.

*Get students started in the texts they select.* Students who are inexperienced at reading may need help getting hooked on a book and sticking with it. What the teacher can do to help is to offer even simple kinds of support such as reading aloud the first few pages of a book to the student until the student is engaged enough to continue on his own. Similarly, the teacher and student might alternate reading pages before the student is left alone to read. Think about how long it takes you to get hooked on a novel or an article you are reading. Some students just need some company, discussion, and support to get to the point where they have an internal desire to just keep reading.

*Help students overcome reading dilemmas they encounter when reading on their own.* We typically think of skills and strategy instruction as something that occurs during whole-class times. Unfortunately, not all students benefit from the same instruction at the same time. "Running alongside" readers (Bomer, 1999) as they read independently gives teachers an opportunity to not only help students make sense of the text they choose but also teach something about the comprehension process. Keeping in mind that the purpose here is to help facilitate students' reading rather than to interrupt it, teachers might use this time judiciously with individuals to teach students strategies for figuring out word pronunciations and meanings as problems come up in the reading and to model strategies for comprehension through thinking aloud and making their *own* reading processes explicit. (p. 108)

✳ ✳ ✳ ✳ ✳ ✳

As you reflect on the importance of time spent "just reading", think about something you have learned to do well and that you enjoy. What about driving? It is difficult to imagine becoming a versatile and proficient driver without getting behind the wheel regularly, driving on different roads in a variety of weather conditions, and experiencing an array of traffic situations. You could learn the rules of the road, consider strategies for hypothetical driving dilemmas, or even practice various components of driving, such as starting a car or using a clutch. Without selecting your own destination, sitting in the driver's seat, and learning from on-the-spot decisions along the way, it is doubtful that you would have ever become a confident, competent driver. Likewise, studying the reading process and examining skills and strategies without setting students free to read will ensure that students remain inexperienced as readers and unlikely to attempt increasingly diverse and sophisticated texts. The "opportunity to read" standard should top the list of instructional priorities in secondary schools.

# 4

# Interventions and Support for Struggling Adolescents

What is your school's plan to address the needs of students with the most severe reading and writing difficulties? Consider how you would respond to the following three students, all of whom could be found in most middle and high schools across a range of communities.

Allison is a 6th grader in a regular classroom. According to informal assessments, she reads at approximately a 2nd grade level. She received Title I reading assistance until she began 4th grade, the grade level at which her school district stopped providing supplemental services. Between 4th grade and 6th grade, without any extra help, she experienced minimal growth in literacy. At the same time, the texts she was expected to negotiate were becoming more complex as the curriculum in middle school was focused on specific content standards. The literacy gaps between Allison and other students and the mismatch between what Allison could read comfortably and what she was assigned to read were growing wider by the day.

Eduard is a 7th grade student who moved to the United States from El Salvador at age 8. Although he was placed in 2nd grade at that time, he had no prior schooling. Although Eduard's competency in the English language had developed remarkably by 7th grade, he was still frustrated when reading 1st-grade-level materials, and writing was even more difficult. Eduard began the year on a regular academic team, but by late fall of the year, he was moved back to the school's English as a second language (ESL) team. Even with this level of support, no noticeable change occurred in Eduard's literacy skills. The courses in this special program centered mostly on language development, with little attention to literacy.

Michael is a 10th grade student who is identified as mildly mentally retarded. He does not yet read or write anything comfortably. Simple picture books with four or five words per page sometimes confuse him, and getting Michael to even pick up a pencil to attempt writing is a formidable challenge to his teachers. In addition to two periods of special education, Michael is mainstreamed into two additional courses: Food/Nutrition and Drama. This makes up his entire school day, given that his school is on a block schedule and all students take four classes per term. The teachers of these regular academic track courses complain that Michael cannot manage the reading and writing demands of their subjects, despite his interest in hands-on activities. The special education courses would appear to help build his literacy competence, but this is not the case. His reading class has 20 students, all with very different profiles as readers and writers, and instruction is rarely personalized to meet individual developmental needs. Instead, the majority of time is spent in whole-class, large-group instruction. This is not unusual. As Vaughn, Moody, and Schumm (1998) reported from their research findings, the special education reading resource room commonly focuses on whole-class instruction, with very little, if any, differentiated instruction. In addition, Michael's resource class focuses mainly on helping him keep up with his regular courses rather than improving reading and writing skills.

Chances are, you know of students like Allison, Eduard, and Michael. Although these three students may be classified differently in school, either as regular academic track, ESL, or special education students, they are all quite similar from a literacy development perspective. All three have the potential to grow as readers and writers, but likely none of them will have all of their needs met within typical larger instructional settings, despite our best efforts to create classrooms that are responsive to every student. We know that students need access to a rich and rigorous curriculum and that segregated education does not work (see Fisher, Sax, & Pumpian, 1999; Ivey, 2004; Kennedy & Fisher, 2001). Students such as Allison, Eduard, and Michael need academic support in their content classes as well as intervention to improve their literacy performance. In other words, they are all good candidates for high-quality supplemental instruction.

In this chapter we help you consider the nature and purposes of effective intervention for secondary students. As you read, we urge you to think beyond "program" as a commercially available product. Although we do not wish to advocate an across-the-board rejection of purchasable reading programs, we do want readers of this book to consider, first, what high-quality interventions accomplish. The essential question that guides our thinking about literacy interventions is this:

*Do the intervention initiatives cause students to read more and to read better?*

As you read this chapter, pay attention to the five major areas that support this essential question. If you do not currently have an intervention in place, use these guiding principles to develop your framework. If you already have a special program for struggling readers and writers, use the principles to evaluate your efforts and to revise them accordingly. If you are using a packaged reading program, consider which of the areas are adequately addressed in your program and what additional changes you will need to adequately address all of these vital areas.

We begin with a short consideration of why we continue to see students with persistent reading and writing problems into the middle grades and beyond despite such a strong emphasis on literacy acquisition in the early grades during the past several decades. Next, we address the five major areas supporting our essential guiding question.

## Reasons for Persistent Reading Problems Among Secondary School Students

It never fails to happen. At some point in the middle of the semester in our courses with preservice secondary teachers, some all-too-familiar questions are asked: "I don't mean to sound like it's not my job to take responsibility for this, but why in the world would I get students in my 10th grade World History course who still read on a 3rd grade level? Shouldn't the elementary school teachers have taken care of that? Why did they keep passing these kids on to the next grade level?" We imagine that some veteran teachers who still struggle to help low-achieving readers secretly ask themselves the same questions.

We believe these complex questions have no simple answers. We have known a range of struggling readers whose difficulties could be attributed to a wide variety of personal, social, cultural, and academic histories, some perhaps controllable by school instruction and some not. Some specific students we know illustrate the bevy of possibilities.

Perla is a 9th grader who moved to the United States from Mexico during the middle of 8th grade. Although she has some Spanish literacy skills, her experience with print in general is minimal. She reported that in her Mexican school, there were no books, and reading had been limited to what the teacher wrote on the chalkboard. She is learning to speak, comprehend, read, and write English all at the same time.

Melissa, a 6th grader reading most comfortably in materials at the 1st grade level, has been in 10 different schools since starting kindergarten because her mother has difficulty finding permanent full-time work and moves frequently for job opportunities. Melissa has not been in one classroom with consistent instruction and experiences long enough to learn to read and write.

Ryan is an 8th grade student with a great attitude and no apparent learning difficulties. He has been in the same school district since kindergarten and has no personal or family issues that would hinder his progress in reading and writing. In fact, he receives significant support from his parents, including their participation in school activities, constant communication with Ryan's teachers, and a limitless supply of books at home for pleasure reading. Nevertheless, Ryan still reads at approximately the 4th grade level. Whatever worked with other students in Ryan's classes across the years did not work for Ryan.

Although individual situations are complex and varied, we can point to some specific and often widespread reasons for persistent reading difficulties. First, many of the students who come to middle and high school as struggling readers were assigned as younger students to remedial reading programs that are known to focus on decontextualized skills, literal recall, and skills worksheets at the expense of purposeful, strategic, silent reading experiences (Johnston & Allington, 1991). This kind of instruction has been tied to slowing rather than accelerating reading progress (Johnston & Allington, 1991). Thus struggling readers fall further and further behind their peers.

Second, students who do not read well read less and consequently do not get any better at reading (Stanovich, 1986). Related to this situation, students who experience failure at reading and writing year after year lose motivation and feel helpless to improve (Johnston & Winograd, 1985). Many of these students come to believe that reading and writing are unattainable goals. It is ironic that students who most need the benefits of reading connected text get many fewer opportunities than the good readers who are reading more not only during the school day but also outside of school (Anderson, Wilson, & Fielding, 1988).

Third, school reading alone may limit the reading experiences of all students, and this is especially detrimental to the most inexperienced readers. Secondary schools rely mainly on common textbooks and anthologies for the whole class, despite their inappropriateness for meeting individual needs (Alvermann & Moore, 1991). Grade-level textbooks are typically too hard for struggling readers, but that is not the only issue. Even if students could read textbooks and anthologies fluently and with understanding, we do not know of any containing enough text to offer the volume of experiences students need to become even mildly expert at reading. Every textbook needs to be supplemented with trade books; newspaper, magazine, and journal articles; Internet sites; and the like. Struggling readers might actually choose to read more if they had access to readable, high-interest texts, but secondary schools often do not make available the texts that students prefer to read. (Worthy, Moorman, & Turner, 1999).

Fourth, to make progress, many students just need continued instruction in reading beyond the elementary grades. Unfortunately, although the range and complexity of texts students must negotiate increase as they progress into middle and high school, the amount of instruction and support for reading and writing actually decreases. Even when students get support for learning specific content, they might not get experiences that actually help them get better at reading and writing in general. We know of English teachers who are exceptional at helping low-achieving students understand the theme of a Shakespearean play, but these same students may leave the class with no better understanding of how to read and make sense of even much easier materials on their own.

We cannot possibly trace the precise origins of students' reading difficulties, and on an individual level it seems nonproductive to place blame on earlier home or school experiences. What we can do is design solid, evidence-based interventions for students who need something extra. We now turn to some critical issues in planning extra help in reading and writing.

## Replacing the Quick Fix with Effective Interventions

Envision this classroom scene. A 6th grade teacher stands before all of her students, each of whom has a copy of a workbook. The teacher makes the sound for the letter *B*, and then the whole class repeats in unison, "Buh, Buh, Buh." Next, they move to the letter *C*: "Cuh, Cuh, Cuh." Wait! "Sss, Sss, Sss." They continue on through the alphabet until they have dutifully completed the daily 15 minutes of phonics instruction required by their district. The teacher rolls her eyes and sighs almost apologetically to her students as she leads the drill she has been instructed to conduct. Reading scores were devastatingly low in this rural school during the previous year, and a district-level decision had been made to remediate all students just to "cover the bases." All English teachers were invited to one 45-minute meeting at which they were handed a teacher's manual to read on their own and then ordered to go forth and conquer the enemy. Is this scene far-fetched? Exaggerated? We wish that were the case.

We have stumbled across episodes like this one in several secondary schools during the past 10 years. More often than not, it happens in schools with low reading achievement in search of a quick fix. It is hard to know where to begin when listing everything wrong with this scene. For starters, it is quite (no, very) likely that no one in the room still needs work with basic letter-sound correspondences. For sure, not everyone in the room needs the same developmental instruction. It is easy to imagine what might be running through the minds of students in this class reading comfortably at and above their grade level. No one is complaining, though, because this lesson is a no-brainer, and it is certainly more bearable than a round-robin reading of a teacher-selected classic novel (see Chapter 1). Second, do any of the students, or even the teacher, know how this lesson connects to real reading and writing? We don't. Third, the workbooks accompanying this program cost the district more than $25 per student. With 300 students in 6th grade at this school alone, this is a substantial investment with little evidence that it will make the slightest difference. Chances are, it will not.

Less extreme, more expensive, but similarly futile attempts to "remediate" reading problems have surfaced in even more schools where reading programs of questionable theoretical soundness are adopted and teachers and administrators cross their fingers that *this one* will work. Often the neediest students are singled out for intervention, but sometimes these students are passed over in favor of the infamous 25th-to-50th-percentile group who show greater potential for making progress (or at least for positively affecting schoolwide reading scores). What you might see in these scenarios are students sitting at computers, using workbooks, or being assigned to the least qualified teachers in the school.

Independent research on popular reading programs is incredibly slim. Don't get us wrong, though. Company Web sites are filled with lists of research studies on their products, but you will notice that most of this evidence is offered up by the company itself or by individuals who are identified as authors of the products or who have financial links to the products. That's not to say that these programs are indeed ineffective. The point is that if you want to make an informed decision about what interventions make sense, you have to do your own homework.

We turn now to the five critical areas for you to consider when developing, selecting, or revising interventions for the struggling readers and writers in your secondary school. The guiding question for this chapter, as you will recall, is this:

*Do the intervention initiatives cause students to read more and to read better?*

## Integral Involvement of Expert Teachers

| AREA 4: INTERVENTION AND SUPPORT FOR STRUGGLING READERS  <br> *4. Do the intervention initiatives cause students to read more and to read better?* | | | | | |
|---|---|---|---|---|---|
| | **5** | **4** | **3** | **2** | **1** |
| **4.1. Teachers are actively involved in providing intervention and support.** | Teachers have significant involvement in the design and delivery of the intervention. | | Teachers have some oversight, but the majority of the program is delivered by volunteers or paraprofessionals. | | Teachers have limited or no involvement; intervention is delivered in the absence of a teacher (e.g., via computer-only programs or take-home workbooks). |

If schools are going to make a difference with struggling readers, then they must make it possible for the best teachers to get up close and personal with those readers on an individual level. We know that teachers who are effective at reaching low-achieving readers spend most of their time working one-to-one or in small groups rather than with the whole class at once (Allington & Johnston, 2002; Taylor, Pearson, Clark, & Walpole, 2000). You will hear claims that certain software programs offer individualized instruction, but it is unlikely that a computer could accurately evaluate a student's strengths and needs or respond to the complexity of adolescents' motivations for reading and writing (Alvermann & Rush, 2004).

If your goal is to get students to read more and to read better, no one is in a better position to do so than a teacher who not only knows individual students but also has the opportunity to adjust the instructional context accordingly. Think of a middle or high school student you know whose reading still approximates that of an elementary school student. Chances are that student has had his share of workbooks or the faddish program of the year (year after year) and has spent much time with a plethora of computer programs. What has not likely happened is substantial, recurring instructional time with expert teachers, outside of monitoring and assessment.

Teacher involvement in designing and implementing worthwhile interventions should resemble what Bomer (1999) calls "running alongside" a reader, which we mentioned in Chapter 3. This differs from a conference in that it involves responsive teaching rather than just assessing student progress. An example from our experience helps to illustrate this. Sixth grader Allison is reading Paula Fox's *Monkey Island* (1993) with her teacher. Allison has just read that the homeless character Clay and his homeless friends refuse to go to a shelter to sleep. Here is a look at their conversation:

| | |
|---|---|
| *Allison:* | I was going to say something I didn't understand. Oh, why don't they go to the shelter home? |
| *Teacher:* | What do you think? |
| *Allison:* | 'Cause they can't sleep. |
| *Teacher:* | When I don't understand something, I like to go back and reread. Let's go back to the middle of page 32. It says a nurse in the clinic told them they ought to go to a shelter because of Calvin's arthritis, just like you said. "Better to get arthritis than to get his head bashed in." |
| *Allison:* | So what happened? |
| *Teacher:* | Now why do you think he wouldn't go to a shelter? |
| *Allison:* | 'Cause he might get beat up and get all his clothes stolen. |
| *Teacher:* | I've never been to a shelter. |
| *Allison:* | We go visit shelters. I think we was in 4th grade. I was over my auntie's house, and the [group from the recreation center] went to the shelter, |

> and we went to visit them. And we gave them money and stuff. They got a TV. Kids have, like, little baths and stuff. It's like a big old house, and there be a lot of crooks there.

In our scenario, it is easy to see the value of the teacher's involvement. First, it was possible for this teacher to assess what was confusing the student and holding up her comprehension. Allison clearly needed reminders that looking back at the text is a good way to clear up misunderstandings, and the teacher was able to address this on the spot. Second, the teacher learns additional information about Allison's comprehension, including some strengths that might go unnoticed otherwise. In this episode and others, Allison showed tremendous expertise with connecting information from her real life and drawing inferences to make sense of the texts she reads.

We know of programs in which a student might be asked to read a similar book (or excerpt) and then answer recall questions about it on the computer. What Allison might learn from that experience is a mystery. Furthermore, all we could judge when she finished was whether she could answer comprehension questions. No actual instruction or any real assessment would have occurred. Likewise, we can imagine Allison being handed a worksheet or a packet on drawing inferences because it is part of a scope and sequence of activities in a reading program, in spite of the fact that this is something she already does automatically in real reading. Ironically, she may fail to provide correct answers on the worksheet because it requires her to consider the role of inference-making within short, contrived passages or within a series of unrelated sentences rather than a larger meaningful text that makes sense to her.

In short, intervention without a teacher is hit-or-miss. What you might be asking yourself is how teachers can find time to spend with individual struggling readers during the school day. One-to-one tutoring from expert teachers is an effective but very expensive initiative (Allington, 2004). Moving personnel and resources around is a good start. Broaddus and Bloodgood (1999) describe an elementary school tutoring program that freed classroom teachers from whole-class responsibilities to work one-to-one for a period of time each day. We know there are middle and high schools whose structures allow for this kind of flexibility. For those that do not, however, it will be important to envision interventions that at least allow teachers to get near students and participate with them in literacy experiences. Good interventions include the teacher in a substantial instructional role.

## A Comprehensive Approach to Reading and Writing

| AREA 4: INTERVENTION AND SUPPORT FOR STRUGGLING READERS | | | | | |
|---|---|---|---|---|---|
| 4. Do the intervention initiatives cause students to read more and to read better? | | | | | |
| | **5** | **4** | **3** | **2** | **I** |
| 4.2. Intervention reflects a comprehensive approach to reading and writing. | Intervention is comprehensive and integrated such that students experience reading and writing as a cohesive whole. | | Intervention includes important components of the reading processes but addresses them separately (e.g., 15 minutes of word study followed by an unrelated comprehension activity); either reading or writing is addressed, but not both. | | Intervention focuses on an isolated skill (e.g., topic sentence) or singular aspect of literacy development (e.g., phonics, phonemic awareness, fluency, vocabulary, comprehension). |

One of the pitfalls of reading programs for older students is that they often assume that reading difficulties can be linked to specific deficiencies in basic skills, and more often than not, to word-level or sound-level skills. We know that many students in the middle grades and beyond are still learning to read the words, and we fully support the notion that these students should be taught to do so. However, knowing how to read the words does not necessarily mean that students will be able to read with comprehension, and it certainly does not guarantee that students will choose to read.

We know of middle and high schools that adopt phonics and phonemics awareness programs as supplemental instruction for struggling readers. Just how helpful is this? Although phonics and phonemic awareness were two of the components of the learning-to-read process studied by the National Reading Panel (2000), these fundamental skills probably should not play a major role in secondary interventions (Ivey & Baker, 2004). Phonemic awareness—the knowledge that words are composed of sequences of individual sounds—is probably something most older struggling readers already understand. Likewise, phonics instruction, which focuses on letter-sound correspondence in reading and spelling, was shown to have diminishing effects beyond the 1st grade level. Neither phonics nor phonemic awareness instruction leads to increased comprehension abilities for older students. Even older struggling readers who can read 1st- to 2nd-grade-level materials would receive limited benefits from intensive phonics instruction per se. Struggling readers' work with words needs to be interactive and connected to real texts students are reading and writing.

When we caution teachers and administrators not to put all of their stock into programs that focus on singular aspects of the reading process (such as phonics or fluency), we are often approached by a few teachers who argue that they get strong results with these programs. When questioned further, all will admit that students' learning is mainly limited to reading isolated words. In other words, if you asked these same students to take a test of comprehension, or better yet, asked them to read from their content area books, you would probably see no real improvement in their reading. It is not surprising that a program designed to improve word-calling skills would help students with word calling.

One belief underlying some reading intervention programs is that once students learn to read the words, then they can work on making sense of what they read. We know of programs in which students are given no real texts to read for the first two years of the intervention. We know that time spent reading is a differentiating factor between good and poor readers, and this is just another example of how we inadvertently widen the achievement gaps between students. Good interventions work simultaneously on and make connections between all dimensions of reading and writing. Students should always read and write meaningful texts from the onset of instruction while working on necessary skills and strategies within those experiences. Imagine how much growth students would make via a comprehensive intervention versus a plan that builds skills slowly and piece by piece. Students need the big picture.

An example helps to clarify the point that reading interventions must be comprehensive. Chad is a 7th grade student who reads most comfortably at the 2nd grade level. He is interested in animal camouflage (which also just happens to be relevant to the 7th grade science standards in his school). As part of his intervention, his teacher has collected a group of books on this topic (see Figure 4.1), which he is reading.

---

### FIGURE 4.1
### Easy Books on Animal Camouflage

---

Birchall, B. (1996). *How animals hide.* Bothell, WA: The Wright Group.
Fowler, A. (1997). *Hard to see animals.* Chicago: The Children's Press.
Heller, R. (1995). *How to hide a meadow frog and other amphibians.* New York: Grosset & Dunlap.
Luhrs, R. J. (1996). *Camouflage.* Bothell, WA: The Wright Group.
Otto, C. (1996). *What color is camouflage?* New York: HarperTrophy.

---

When his teacher reads with him, she models and explains comprehension strategies such as connecting prior knowledge about animal camouflage that help her make sense of the text at hand. For example, she says, "I can picture in my mind what the book says about crocodiles swimming underwater to hide because I remember seeing an alligator do the same thing once. It helps to think about things I already know." When Chad reads alone, he collects interesting facts in a reading log that he will later use to write his own text—a picture book for others to read that follows a recurring syntactic pattern:

> If you're an insect, you sit on a stick.
> If you're a tiger, you hide in the grass.

For word study, Chad needs to study common long-vowel patterns in words. He has been sorting words with long-*i* sounds (see Bear, Invernizzi, Templeton, & Johnston, 2003), so to expand and contextualize his understanding of these patterns, he revisits the books on camouflage he has been reading and conducts a word hunt for long-*i* words. He finds the following and records them in his word study notebook:

| hide | light | by |
|------|-------|------|
| time | fight | try |
| wide | might | fly |
| like |       | why |
| vine |       |      |

In addition, Chad keeps a running list of new vocabulary words he has noticed multiple times across the related texts: *predator, prey, camouflage, chameleon.*

Think about how much Chad is learning about reading and writing in this scenario. Now compare that to working within a program that focuses on sounds, letters, words, or even comprehension strategies presented one at a time. Plus, consider all the instructional time that is wasted when reading and writing are presented piecemeal. Struggling readers in middle and high school do not have this kind of time to waste.

## Reading and Writing That Engages Students

| AREA 4: INTERVENTION AND SUPPORT FOR STRUGGLING READERS<br>*4. Do the intervention initiatives cause students to read more and to read better?* | | | | | |
|---|---|---|---|---|---|
| | **5** | **4** | **3** | **2** | **1** |
| 4.3. Intervention reading and writing is engaging. | Authentic children's and adolescent literature (fiction and nonfiction) is at the core of the intervention. | | Intervention relies on isolated paragraphs on topics selected by the intervention program. | | Program uses artificial text, no connected text-skills work. |

A student sits at a computer staring at a passage on rainforests from a reading software program. Flashy music plays in the background, and if the student has difficulty with a word, he can click on that word for a pronunciation and a definition. After the reading, the program displays a multiple-choice test about the passage. The student gets immediate feedback on each response, and he can return to the text at any time to reread the portion of the text containing the information relevant to each item.

Now, take away the music and the clickable features and what do you have? It's a textbook passage. It's easy to find a program like this one but difficult to ascertain what students learn about reading or writing from such a program. Having students read and answer questions to check their understanding is certainly not a new idea, even if it is packaged in an attractive software program. Such routines have never been useful in helping to improve students' reading. More important, they do anything but make students want to read more.

For students who have experienced unsuccessful, painful literacy experiences, perhaps the worst thing we can do is inundate them with difficult and lifeless reading and writing tasks that bear no resemblance to the reading and writing they encounter in the real world. Effective instruction for all adolescents focuses on their individual interests and incorporates diverse reading materials such as trade books and the digital texts they read on their own (Alvermann, 2002). It is difficult to find a study of adolescent literacy these days that does not somehow point to the importance of engagement and particularly to using engaging texts (see Ivey & Broaddus, 2001; Worthy, Moorman, & Turner, 1999). For students who still finding reading difficult, relevant texts are especially critical.

Although much attention has been paid lately to the role of students' out-of-school literacy experiences (such as e-mail, video games, songwriting, and religious-based reading and writing), what interests individual students spans the gamut of possibilities, including many school-related topics (Ivey & Broaddus, 2001). Kenny, an 11th grade student reading comfortably in 5th-grade-level materials, was intrigued by World War II, and his teacher designed a reading and writing program based on high-interest books that were manageable for him (see Figure 4.2). Annie, a 7th grade student with learning disabilities who receives special education services, read a series of books by Roald Dahl after finishing *The Magic Finger* (Dahl, 1966), the first book she had ever read from cover to cover. Students in one middle school tutoring program selected high-interest, humorous picture books to practice and read aloud to their peers in a readers theater celebration (see Figure 4.3).

Engagement in literacy is possible even for students who do not yet read published materials comfortably because of extremely limited knowledge of

---

### FIGURE 4.2
### Intermediate-Level Books on World War II Combat

Dowsel, P. (2003). *Pearl Harbor (Days that shook the world)*. New York: Steck-Vaughn.
Elliott, L. M. (2001). *Under a war-torn sky*. New York: Hyperion.
Hipperson, C. E. (2001). *The belly gunner*. Brookfield, CT: Twenty-First Century Books.
Platt, R. (2004). *D-Day landings: The story of the allied invasion*. New York: DK Publishing.
Tanaka, S. (2001). *Attack on Pearl Harbor: The true story of the day America entered World War II*. New York: Hyperion.
Tanaka, S. (2004). *D-Day: A day that changed America*. New York: Hyperion.

---

**FIGURE 4.3**
**Humorous Picture Books for Readers Theater**

---

Cronin, D. (2000). *Click, clack, moo: Cows that type.* New York: HarperCollins.
Cronin, D. (2003). *Diary of a worm.* New York: HarperCollins.
Scieszka, J., & Smith, L. (1998). *Squids will be squids.* New York: Viking.
Scieszka, J., & Smith, L. (2004). *Science verse.* New York: Viking.
Teague, M. (2002). *Dear Mrs. LaRue: Letters from obedience school.* New York: Scholastic.
Willems, M. (2003). *Don't let the pigeon drive the bus!* New York: Hyperion.

---

reading and writing. Consider the case of Robbie, who was frustrated in reading 1st-grade-level books and was generally bored by the patterned texts he could read fluently. Robbie dictated to his teacher captions about his favorite characters from a Web-based cartoon (www.homestarrunner.com):

> Homestar said, "Whatcha doing?" Strong Mad, Strong Bad, and The Cheat just stared at him.

His teacher wrote his words, and then Robbie matched up his text with images of characters from the cartoon that he located on the Internet. He reviewed each line of text to make sure it made sense and then created a book about the cartoon that he reread and passed along to friends who also enjoyed this Web site. Not only does Robbie get to read and write about what interests him, but also his teacher has the opportunity to demonstrate for him some conventions of print (such as punctuation) within a text that makes sense to him.

It is easy to spot engaging instruction within an intervention. Students are eager to read and write. They talk about what they read and write. They read and write real texts. They come into class ready to begin, and when the period is over, it is difficult to get them to put down their texts. Typically, engaging literacy experiences extend far beyond one class period.

A not-so-engaging intervention is just as easy to detect. Students are distracted or intent just on "getting it done." There is limited talk around the literacy experiences (but perhaps much "off-task" talk). Real reading and writing is nonexistent or limited to short, contrived passages. The intervention consists of a series of brief, isolated lessons.

As you select or design a plan to improve students' reading and writing, let what engages students be the heart of your program.

## Interventions Based on Useful and Relevant Assessments

| AREA 4: INTERVENTION AND SUPPORT FOR STRUGGLING READERS<br>4. Do the intervention initiatives cause students to read more and to read better? | | | | | |
|---|---|---|---|---|---|
| | **5** | **4** | **3** | **2** | **1** |
| **4.4. Intervention instruction is driven by useful and relevant assessments.** | Teacher-administered assessments are ongoing and are used to tailor individual instruction; writing samples and text-based discussions are one type of assessment used. | | Uniform assessments are used for placement, program entry, and program exit. | | All students start at the same point and move through the intervention components regardless of their individual performance. |

Often, standardized tests are used to place students in special reading programs. Unfortunately, most of these tests do little more than separate the good readers from the poor readers, and seldom do they provide information that helps us actually design appropriate instruction. If test results indicate that a 10th grade student is reading on a 3.5 level, all we know is that there is a lot of catching up to do. Placing this student in a generic instructional program designated for struggling readers does not relieve us of the need to dig deeper to identify this student's strengths and needs in reading and writing.

We, the authors of this book, are literacy researchers, teacher educators, and experienced teachers of struggling adolescent learners. However, neither of us would dream of trying to figure out instruction for a low-achieving reader without sensible assessments to guide the way. Initial assessments to help conceptualize useful assessments might include (1) an informal reading inventory (for example, Qualitative Reading Inventory-3, Leslie & Caldwell, 2005) to get a rough estimate of instructional reading level; (2) a developmental spelling inventory (for example, Bear, Invernizzi, Templeton, & Johnston, 2003) to evaluate levels of word knowledge; (3) a writing sample; (4) a written response to a teacher read-aloud to examine comprehension; and (5) a survey, questionnaire, or interview about students' previous literacy experiences and preferences. Knowing the critical connections between assessment and instruction, it is difficult to imagine an intervention that places students indiscriminately into an instructional track or sequence. It is also unrealistic to expect satisfactory results from a program in which all students start at the same point and move along at the same pace.

Even with good initial assessments, progress can be sustained only through ongoing evaluations in which teachers carefully examine student responses and participation in reading and writing and then adjust materials and instruction accordingly to ensure continued participation and improvement (Johnston, 1987). The value of informal, ongoing assessments is clarified through the example of Alejandro (Ivey & Broaddus, 2004), an 8th grade ESL learner whose initial assessments indicated that he was frustrated at the 1st grade reading level and that he had rudimentary knowledge of common spelling patterns (*bet* for *bed; chap* for *ship*). He had excellent listening comprehension that he was able to demonstrate orally, but he struggled to write anything.

A first look at Alejandro's assessments provided a good start. He appeared to benefit from supported reading in simple pattern books (for example, *This Car* by Paul Collicutt (2002), word study focusing on short-vowel word families (*bat, fat, sat, mat* versus *fan, can, pan, ran*), and writing using a model sentence structure. However, it was difficult to engage Alejandro in reading and writing until his teacher realized that he was interested in books about the solar system and space exploration (for example, *Planets Around the Sun* by Seymour Simon (2002). When reading and writing were linked to a topic of interest to Alejandro, his motivation to learn became more apparent, and understanding the patterns in words and syntactic structures became more important to him. He wanted his own writing to make sense and to appeal to an audience. In the case of Alejandro, as with other students, instruction without useful and relevant assessments would be hit-or-miss. Even solid, teacher-administered initial assessments only get you in the ballpark. It is hard to imagine how Alejandro and students like him would make progress within an intervention that relied on a predetermined set of experiences and activities with no allowance for teacher input or student strengths, interests, and needs.

Perhaps of utmost importance when it comes to assessment is matching students with texts they can read and want to read (see Figure 4.4 for a guide

FIGURE 4.4
**Criteria for Matching Texts with Readers**

| Reading Level | Word Recognition/Comprehension |
|---|---|
| Easy reading/Independent level | 98–100 percent word recognition |
| (For student independent reading) | 90–100 percent comprehension |
| Challenge reading/Instructional level | 95–97 percent word recognition |
| (For reading with support) | 75–89 percent comprehension |
| Difficult reading/Frustration level | Below 90 percent word recognition |
| (Nonproductive, inappropriate) | Below 75 percent comprehension |

*Source:* Adapted from Barr, R., Blachowitz, C. L., & Wogman-Sadow, W. (1995). *Reading diagnosis for teachers: An instructional approach* (3rd ed.). New York, Longman

to judging appropriate reading for individual students). When students can read fluently and with interest, they will read more and read better. If you are starting an intervention, we advise you to make this matching of students and texts your first order of business. Keep in mind, though, that reading level should not be the sole criterion. Prior knowledge and interest play an important part in text readability, and students can often transcend their reading-level scores on informal tests if they have strong experiences with a particular topic. We strongly caution you not to limit students' reading choices to lists of leveled texts that accompany some programs. We have found that these selections rarely match the range and diversity of students' reading preferences and needs.

## Providing Plentiful Opportunities for Authentic Reading and Writing

In Chapter 3 we outlined the reasons that time spent "just reading" during the school day should be a priority for all secondary students. In short, good readers have read more than poor readers. So if we want our poor readers to perform more like our accomplished readers, it makes sense that any worthwhile intervention should have at its core significant opportunities for

| AREA 4: INTERVENTION AND SUPPORT FOR STRUGGLING READERS<br>4. Do the intervention initiatives cause students to read more and to read better? | | | | | |
|---|---|---|---|---|---|
| | **5** | **4** | **3** | **2** | **1** |
| 4.5. Intervention includes significant opportunities for authentic reading and writing. | The majority of intervention time is devoted to authentic reading and writing. | | Periodic opportunities are provided for students to read or write. | | No connected reading and writing is provided or required (e.g., sole focus is on word-level activities or skills worksheets). |

real reading and writing. As we stated at the beginning of this chapter, it is quite possible that special reading programs in our struggling readers' schools have consisted of skill-and-drill work rather than authentic reading and writing.

Work with skills and strategies should *support* actual reading and writing rather than *supplant* it. In Figure 4.5 we offer a sample instructional plan for a 45-minute tutoring session. Notice that a full 40 minutes is devoted to engagement with text (warm-up reading, guided reading, writing), and the remaining five minutes is designated for working with word patterns. In this and all other intervention efforts, skill and strategy work should serve to help students read and write more meaningfully and efficiently, but within a context that students find relevant. Note that attention to reading and writing skills is included within the first three components (such as teacher explanation of strategies), but it is connected to authentic texts, and students attend to these concepts *in the act* of reading and writing.

You can certainly find commercially available programs that promote independent reading, but if you are considering one of these programs, be sure to consider how a ready-made curriculum might actually limit students' reading. Mallette, Henk, and Melnick (2004) studied the effects of *Accelerated Reader* (*AR*) on students' attitudes toward reading. Although *AR* had positive effects on students' attitudes toward academic reading, it made no measurable difference on students' attitudes toward recreational reading. And it actually had a negative influence on the self-perception of low-achieving male readers, who would probably make up a large part of the target intervention population. Keep in mind that *AR* does not include any

FIGURE 4.5
**Lesson Plan for a 45-Minute Tutoring Session**

| Lesson Plan | | |
|---|---|---|
| Component | Tasks/Books Used | Tutor's Notes |
| *Warm-up* (5 minutes)<br>Familiar rereads for fluency. | | |
| *Guided Reading* (20 minutes)<br>• *Before reading:* Introduce book; preview pictures; point out interesting details; discuss what you already know about the topic and predict what the author might tell you.<br>• *During reading:* Have student read; interject to share your own thoughts; clarify confusing parts; ask questions to get students to think ahead; share mental connections you're making, and urge students to do the same.<br>• *After reading:* Have a discussion about where this text leaves you. How did the author help your understanding about this topic? What are you still curious about? Who else would like to read this book and why? | | |
| *Writing* (15 minutes)<br>• *Before writing:* Introduce theme and format of the writing; talk about the purpose of the writing and what it's meant to convey to the audience.<br>• *During writing:* You start first—attempt the writing yourself; share your thought processes and strategies for figuring out what you want to say (this may include some brainstorming/prewriting); write your own piece as the student writes; clarify and provide support and strategies as necessary.<br>• *After writing:* Read to each other. Talk about the process of writing, including what worked for you and what you're still trying to figure out. | | |
| *Word Study* (5 minutes)<br>Select one:<br>• Word sort (Sort words into categories by pattern.)<br>• Word hunt (Search for words that fit a pattern in familiar books.)<br>• Writing sort (Write words into categories according to a pattern.) | | |

instruction in reading and writing, nor does it involve the teacher in a role other than monitoring.

## How Will You Know It's Working?

Real measures of reading improvement are hard to pin down. When students are receiving supplemental instruction in addition to a range of other reading and writing experiences, it is difficult to determine which components of instruction are causing a difference. Some programs come with their own assessments, but these may prove only that students can better perform the tasks required by those particular programs (for example, improving on a test of word recognition following an intensive program focused on word recognition). Such assessment results do not necessarily equate to improved reading and writing.

Given the lack of independent research available on most commercial programs and the unfeasibility of a school conducting its own scientifically validating research, perhaps some more readily observable, informal assessments make sense: Do you notice a difference in your students' reading and writing in their content area classes? Are students more inclined to read on their own? Are students beginning to read harder and more varied materials on their own? Do you notice differences between students participating in the intervention versus students who are not? Do students look forward to the intervention?

Recall Eduard from the beginning of this chapter. Evidence of his success was clear a year and a half into the intervention, which consisted of biweekly, teacher-led tutoring sessions that included lots of reading in high-interest books on his instructional and independent reading levels, modeled writing, and assessment-driven word study. He entered 7th grade barely able to read 1st-grade-level materials, but midway through 8th grade he was often spotted carrying around various chapter books with bookmarks holding his place. While an informal reading inventory suggested he had increased four grade levels, listening to him read and discuss a sophisticated book he had selected was all the proof his teachers needed. Eduard would enter high school as a reader.

# 5

# Leadership and Schoolwide Support for Literacy

You've read about the importance of the English class, you know how content area teachers can use language for learning, you understand that students must be provided with the opportunity to read, and you recognize the importance of intervention initiatives. What's left? What will tie a secondary school's literacy system together? Our remaining question focuses on leadership and schoolwide support. The question that remains is this:

*Is there a schoolwide emphasis on literacy, and does this focus develop teacher expertise?*

To answer this question, we need to focus on a number of factors related to the whole school. As you might have predicted, we are concerned about the access that teachers have to books and technology. We also know that human and fiscal resources must be directed toward the schoolwide literacy initiative if it is to be effective. Further, we understand that professional development, a culture of collaboration, and access to peer coaches make a difference as teachers develop their expertise (International Reading Association, 2006). And finally, we recognize the research on using student performance data to make instructional decisions and school improvement decisions. We start with access to materials for reading and writing.

## Access to Materials

As we have said several times before, teachers must have access to materials in order to teach. Thus the school must regularly budget for purchases of books

| AREA 5: LEADERSHIP AND SCHOOLWIDE SUPPORT | | | | | |
|---|---|---|---|---|---|
| 5. Is there a schoolwide emphasis on literacy, and does this focus develop teacher expertise? | | | | | |
| | **5** | **4** | **3** | **2** | **1** |
| 5.1. All teachers have access to materials for reading and writing. | Funds are regularly expended on books across content areas, developmental reading levels, and students' personal reading preferences, and on technological resources. | | Limited funds are allocated for departments, classroom teachers, or the school library for purchase of books; technology is generally available in classrooms. | | No funds are available for purchase of books; computers are available in a lab. |

and technology. As you might recall, Hoover High School in San Diego spends several hundred dollars each year for each classroom to have a well-stocked library (Fisher, 2004). This expenditure is in addition to the funds for the school library and standards-aligned instructional materials and textbooks. Other schools, such as Thomas Harrison Middle School in Harrisonburg, Virginia, designate thousands of dollars each year to stock a shared collection of books matching students' developmental reading needs and the state's content standards (Ivey, 2002). This collection is in addition to, but also affiliated with, the school's regular library, which is also well stocked and heavily used by students and teachers.

The reasons for making access to books for learning and teaching a priority are countless. We know that having a plentiful supply of books makes a notable difference in early literacy development (Neuman, 1999), and books play an equally significant role in secondary schools. Older students report that, fundamentally, what motivates them to read is good reading materials (Ivey & Broaddus, 2001; Worthy & McKool, 1996). Plus, large-scale studies of exemplary teachers (see, for example, Allington & Johnston, 2002) tell us that good teaching involves matching students and texts (Allington, 2002a). The most effective teachers develop a "multisourced and multileveled curriculum" (Allington, 2002b, p. 18) that cannot be implemented with a single textbook or a set of class novels.

Allington (2001) points out some research-based comparisons of the haves versus the have-nots of book access:

• High-achieving schools have more books in classroom libraries than lower-achieving schools.

• Schools in wealthier neighborhoods have classrooms with richer book collections that those in poorer neighborhoods.

• Classrooms with more books have students who read more often.

• Classrooms with more books have more students reading things that make sense to them. (p. 54)

These are correlational rather than causal relationships, but our guess is that you'll want to err on the side of logic and intuition and go with the theory that more books equals more reading and better reading.

So how many books are enough? Given the range of readers in secondary schools and taking into consideration the academic, cultural, and linguistic diversity among students, along with the breadth and depth of content topics to be covered across the subject areas, a school's collection of books and other materials for reading ought to be vast and expansive, to say the least. In Figure 5.1, we provide a sample of the types of texts that are available (in abundance) for classroom use in the literacy library at Thomas Harrison Middle School.

To meet the individual needs of students designated for special education, English as a second language programs, and special reading programs, this range and quantity of materials—literally thousands of books—is nonnego-

---

**FIGURE 5.1**

**Examples of Categories of Books in the Literacy Library at Thomas Harrison Middle School**

Concept books (easy-to-read materials on topics such as colors, seasons, and American symbols for beginning-level ESL students)

Easy informational picture books (high-interest but accessible texts for struggling readers)

Easy fictional picture books (high-interest but accessible texts for struggling readers)

Sophisticated picture books used to teach literary concepts (e.g., mood, dialect, and characterization)

Biographies across a range of difficulty levels, both contemporary and historical

Comics and graphic novels

Science informational books connected to state standards (e.g., animal adaptation, cells, gravity, and habitats)

Mathematics informational books connected to state standards (e.g., geometry concepts, using statistics, fractions, and percentages)

History informational books connected to state standards (e.g., Civil War, immigration in the United States, and Revolutionary War)

Series books

Transitional chapter books (easy chapter books for struggling readers who are moving toward reading novels)

Fictional novels (purchased in sets of four or five to be used in literature discussion groups)

tiable. Keep in mind, though, that this attention to books benefits *all* students in the school (Brozo & Hargis, 2003). High-achieving readers and reluctant readers also enjoy access to materials that suit their personal interests and materials that make their content classes more interesting and relevant.

Building this collection of materials to be used as the core of instruction is important enough for administrators to consider allocating time and resources to make it happen. We recommend that administrators designate a team of people—the school's reading specialist, the media specialist, and one representative from each of the subject areas—to examine and compile lists of appropriate materials to begin this process. To get started, suggestions for excellent reading materials can be found on the Web sites of professional organizations connected to the various disciplines (see Figure 5.2). Many

---

**FIGURE 5.2**
**Web Sites for Identifying Trade Books Across the Content Areas**

**National Council of Teachers of English**
www.ncte.org
This site provides tools and resources specific to every teacher from the elementary level through college.

**National Council for the Social Studies (NCSS) Notable Books**
www.socialstudies.org/resources/notable/
This site offers a comprehensive list of social studies literature resources for young people.

**Carol Hurst's Children's Literature Site—Curriculum Areas**
www.carolhurst.com/subjects/curriculum.html
Visitors will find links, ideas, and book titles for using literature in teaching various subject areas.

**Center for the Study of Books in Spanish for Children and Adolescents**
www.csusm.edu/csb/
This site serves as a resource center of books in Spanish and in English about Hispanics/Latinos for children and adolescents. The resources can help improve the effectiveness of seminars, forums, and/or workshops on books in Spanish for children and adolescents.

**Multicultural Reading from Cynthia Leitich Smith Children's Literature Resources**
www.cynthialeitichsmith.com (click on link for "Children and Young Adult Resources")
This site has an annotated bibliography of titles from children's and young adult literature; it is useful for curriculum building, collection diversification, and planning for reading groups. Quick-print format allows easy printing and distribution.

**National Science Teachers Association's Outstanding Science Trade Books**
www.nsta.org/ostbc/
This site features outstanding science trade books chosen by the National Science Teachers Association.

**International Reading Association's (IRA) "Choices" Booklists**
www.reading.org/resources/tools/choices.html
This site features annually published booklists chosen by teachers, children, and young adults.

kinds of materials typically purchased by elementary schools are appropriate for struggling readers in secondary schools, particularly if they offer rich information in a simple-to-read format.

As literacy educators and consultants, we are hesitant even to begin working with schools that are not willing to consider the importance of having ample materials for reading and writing. Prompted by low reading test scores, school leaders will often ask us to present inservice workshops on teaching specific word-recognition or comprehension strategies. One of our initial responses is, "Do your students have plenty of books they can read and opportunities to read them?" All the strategy instruction in the world will not help build the skill and motivation to read when students do not have access to an abundance of interesting, manageable texts.

## Use of Human Resources

| AREA 5: LEADERSHIP AND SCHOOLWIDE SUPPORT 5. Is there a schoolwide emphasis on literacy, and does this focus develop teacher expertise? | | | | | |
|---|---|---|---|---|---|
| | **5** | **4** | **3** | **2** | **1** |
| 5.2. Human resources are dedicated to the schoolwide literacy plan. | Reading specialists serve as literacy instructional leaders across the curriculum; there is a schoolwide literacy council that meets regularly to establish policies and procedures related to literacy. | | Reading resource teachers or a reading specialist works with a limited number of students in pullout programs; the literacy council has no authority and meets infrequently. | | There are no certified reading specialists, and there is no literacy council supported by the administration. |

It is difficult to imagine a middle school or a high school making notable strides in literacy achievement without a designated staff member whose sole responsibility is to worry about students' reading and writing development. Sadly, we know of many, many secondary schools employing no one with expertise in literacy. We agree with the International Reading Association's position that a reading specialist—a role most often associated with elementary schools—should play a prominent instructional leadership role *even* in middle and high schools (International Reading Association, 2000).

What would a secondary school reading specialist do? The roles of reading specialists in general have changed over time (Bean, Cassidy, Grumet, Shelton, & Wallis, 2002), from serving mainly as remedial reading teachers working with individuals or with small groups of students, to serving as reading diagnosticians, to serving in advisory or consulting roles to regular classroom teachers. Bean, Swan, and Knaub (2003) tell us that currently reading specialists in exemplary programs serve their schools in the following capacities:

- *Resource to classroom teachers* (e.g., sharing ideas for struggling readers, modeling effective literacy instruction, and leading professional book discussion groups)
- *Liaison to school and community* (e.g., consulting with administrators on decisions regarding literacy; working with the librarians, speech therapists, volunteers, special educators, and parents)
- *Coordinator of the reading program* (e.g., assisting in writing of curriculum, identifying and collecting reading materials and other instructional materials, maintaining literacy center or location for literacy materials)
- *Contributor to assessment* (e.g., helping to select and develop assessments, conducting assessments with individuals or small groups of students, interpreting assessment results with teachers and parents)
- *Instructor* (e.g., teaching individual struggling readers or small groups, working in pullout or in-class settings)

All these responsibilities seem crucial when looking at schoolwide literacy achievement, so can you imagine how any of it gets accomplished without at least one full-time reading specialist?

To give you an idea of the critical nature of this position, let us take you through the day of one middle school reading specialist we know. Laura begins her day at 8:00 a.m. in the school cafeteria, where she greets a group of 20 preservice teachers from a local university who help her run a twice-weekly tutoring program for struggling readers. Laura has prepared, as she does before each session, individual lesson plans for the 20 tutors and their tutees based on student assessments; the plans include books for guided reading, poetry for fluency practice, a writing prompt, and a word-study activity. As tutoring pairs go about the business of reading and writing, Laura moves around the room troubleshooting with individual students and modeling good instruction for the preservice teachers. Next, she meets with the school librarian to review a new order for trade books connected to a 7th grade science curriculum standard—animal and plant evolution. They are careful to select only the most engaging books that match the developmental range of students in this particular school, with reading levels spanning from below the 1st grade level through the high school level.

Laura then travels down the hall for a 90-minute language arts class. She is modeling for the classroom teacher the use of picture books to teach important literary concepts. She reads aloud to students *Voices in the Park* (Browne, 1998), in which four different characters recount their unique perspective on the same park visit. Laura leads students in examining how each character's viewpoint differs through a graphic organizer detailing each character's purpose and feelings and what caught each character's attention. Tomorrow she will return with another picture book, *Rose Blanche* (Gallaz & Innocenti, 1985) that features a shift in perspective midway through the text.

During the lunch break, Laura meets with her principal to review applications for a faculty opening in 8th grade language arts. With the heavy population of second-language learners and special education students in this school, Laura and her principal are keenly aware of the need to identify the candidate with the most experience and qualifications for reaching struggling readers and writers.

After lunch, Laura works with the two other reading specialists at the school to review mid-year literacy assessments that were administered to all students during the previous week. In particular, they are interested in how much progress struggling readers in the morning tutoring program have made, according to an informal reading inventory, in comparison with students at similar achievement levels who are not participating in the program. As the day ends, Laura is on the Internet searching for articles and other professional readings on using writing to learn mathematics, which she will share next week at a meeting of 6th grade math teachers who want to incorporate more literacy experiences into their teaching.

We can remember a time when reading specialists were criticized by regular classroom teachers as having only to work with a handful of students at a time in traditional pullout groups. It was never the case that a reading specialist's job was so simple, but consider all of the balls Laura is juggling. Keep in mind that such a complex set of responsibilities took time to learn to manage and to be able to do thoughtfully and productively. Make no mistake, though: the work of Laura and others like her is absolutely vital to making long-term schoolwide changes in literacy achievement.

## Professional Development

| AREA 5: LEADERSHIP AND SCHOOLWIDE SUPPORT | | | | | |
|---|---|---|---|---|---|
| 5. Is there a schoolwide emphasis on literacy, and does this focus develop teacher expertise? | | | | | |
| | **5** | **4** | **3** | **2** | **1** |
| 5.3. Professional development builds teacher knowledge and expertise. | Professional development opportunities are differentiated and job embedded, focus on increasing knowledge about literacy processes and development, and respect the teacher as a professional. | | Professional development opportunities focus on literacy but are mandated and common for all teachers. | | Professional development centers on learning about programs or textbooks. |

We know that student success is highly dependent on the knowledge, skills, and disposition of teachers (Joyce & Showers, 2002). Teachers have different strengths and needs, just like students. It is hard to imagine a school in which all teachers know the same amount about the same things. Teachers require and deserve professional development that respects their prior knowledge and skills and extends their expertise in the field.

Like other professionals, teachers develop and hone their skills over time (see Wong, 2004). You are probably not the same teacher you were during your first year, but you had to have that first year just like the rest of us. Steffy and Wolfe (2001) and Steffy, Wolfe, Pasch, and Enz (2000) suggest that teachers develop through a series of six stages. Let's explore each of these stages with the idea that we will have to plan professional development for all of them.

**Novice.** The first phase, novice, begins when a prospective teacher enters a formal program of study, such as a teaching credential program or an internship. Of course, all novices begin their program of study with different experiences and backgrounds. This phase focuses on initiating a systematic study of teaching and learning that is likely absent from their collective backgrounds.

**Apprentice.** The apprentice phase begins when a teacher assumes responsibility for instructing a group of students alone. The apprentice needs support and guidance as he makes instructional decisions. Classroom management and classroom routines often consume the time and energy of the apprentice. This phase continues for the first few years of teaching, usually through an induction support program.

**Professional.** The professional phase occurs as teachers become increasingly confident in their instruction and decisions. Teachers at the professional phase have clearly established routines and relationships with students. The professional teacher is willing to share her knowledge with novices and apprentices.

**Expert.** The expert teacher is one who has a vast knowledge base from which to operate. The expert makes decisions thoughtfully and skillfully and is available to assist others in planning instruction or examining student work. The goal is to ensure that every teacher has the opportunity to attain expert status.

**Distinguished.** This phase is reserved for the teachers' teacher—people for whom teaching seems effortless, people we all enjoy watching and might even applaud at the end of a lesson. Distinguished teachers exceed expectations and are regularly called upon for their perspective on local, state, or national education issues.

**Emeritus.** Emeritus status is reserved for skilled teachers who retire and deserve the respect of society for what they have provided. Often emeritus teachers continue to work with children, as tutors, substitutes, mentors, or as curriculum developers and advisors.

"The critical factor that enables teachers to propel themselves through the career life-cycle phases is the reflection-renewal-growth cycle" (Steffy & Wolfe, 2001, p. 18). By this, they mean that teacher development is facilitated when individuals consider what they know or what they are learning and apply it to problems of practice. As Steffy and Wolfe note, teachers at different life stages require different support for their reflections. Although everyone can participate in informational sessions focused on a new instructional strategy or some other topic, what happens after the information has been presented is what really matters. For teachers at the early stages, coaching, peer interaction, portfolio development, and journaling are effective, whereas teacher study groups or learning communities, serving as a peer coach, providing professional development seminars, and the like are especially valuable for veteran teachers (Steffy & Wolfe, 2001, p. 18).

Building on its understanding of the stages that we progress through as professional educators and knowing that different professional development experiences result in different outcomes, the National Staff Development Council (NSDC) identified standards for professional development. All the standards in Figure 5.3 have been designed to meet the following goal: "All

---

**FIGURE 5.3**
**National Staff Development Council Standards for Staff Development**

**Context Standards**

**Staff development that improves the learning of all students:**

• Organizes adults into learning communities whose goals are aligned with those of the school and district.
• Requires skillful school and district leaders who guide continuous instructional improvement.
• Requires resources to support adult learning and collaboration.

**Process Standards**

**Staff development that improves the learning of all students:**

• Uses disaggregated student data to determine adult learning priorities, monitor progress, and help sustain continuous improvement.
• Uses multiple sources of information to guide improvement and demonstrate its impact.
• Prepares educators to apply research to decision making.
• Uses learning strategies appropriate to the intended goal.
• Applies knowledge about human learning and change.
• Provides educators with the knowledge and skills to collaborate.

**Content Standards**

**Staff development that improves the learning of all students:**

• Prepares educators to understand and appreciate all students, create safe, orderly and supportive learning environments, and hold high expectations for their academic achievement.
• Deepens educators' content knowledge, provides them with research-based instructional strategies to assist students in meeting rigorous academic standards, and prepares them to use various types of classroom assessments appropriately.
• Provides educators with knowledge and skills to involve families and other stakeholders appropriately.

*Source:* National Staff Development Council. Copyright 2001 by the National Staff Development Council. Reprinted with permission.

teachers in all schools will experience high-quality professional learning as part of their daily work by 2007." The NSDC Web site provides information about resources for meeting these standards (www.nsdc.org).

## The Culture of Collaboration and Coaching

| AREA 5: LEADERSHIP AND SCHOOLWIDE SUPPORT<br>5. Is there a schoolwide emphasis on literacy, and does this focus develop teacher expertise? | | | | | | | | |
|---|---|---|---|---|---|---|---|---|
| | **5** | **4** | **3** | **2** | **I** |
| 5.4. The school has a culture of collaboration and peer coaching. | Teachers are provided with opportunities to observe and give feedback to one another; teachers are regularly observed sharing ideas and books with one another. | | The school has a peer coach who provides feedback to teachers about their lessons. Teachers meet as departments to plan lessons and discuss their successes. | | Teachers operate as independent contractors and have no opportunities to observe their colleagues. There are no conversations about learning and teaching across classrooms. |

You have no doubt heard that teaching is the second most private thing we do behind closed doors. Although some things should remain private, teaching is not one of them. As Villa, Thousand, and Nevin (2004) note,

> The education profession is well versed in the *lone ranger* way of doing business—one teacher is expected to teach a class of 30 students without support or communication with others. The notion that the so-called self-contained classroom and the lone teacher can somehow meet the ever-increasing needs of a diverse student body is a myth. Only through sharing ideas, materials, resources, and expertise do teachers develop, survive, and thrive. (p. 101)

Yes, collaboration is one of the keys to the success of public schools. Hoy, Tarter, and Kottkamp (1991) developed and tested an organizational climate survey that can be used to identify the openness of a school and areas of need in terms of the collaborative climate.

But how can we make people collaborate? Although the question has many possible answers, including one that focuses on the tone set by the administration, we see promise in peer coaching. We can point to many different models and examples of peer coaching, but in general the results seem to suggest that it improves the collaborative relationships that teachers have with one another and facilitates teacher expertise (Arnau, Kahrs, & Kruskamp, 2004; Herll & O'Drobinak, 2004). Although peer coaching has produced promising results, we also acknowledge that peer coaching could result in contrived collegiality or new administrative and evaluative systems if not carefully and thoughtfully implemented (Lam, Yim, & Lam, 2002).

In growing numbers of schools across the United States, peer coaches are hired to provide resources and professional development for teachers. In some cases, the peer coach is a reading specialist (Bean, 2003); in other cases, the peer coach is a teacher on special assignment (Guiney, 2001). In May 2003, New York City Public Schools posted an ad in *Education Week* seeking "Literacy and Math Coaches." The ad noted that the coaches would "serve as a critical professional development resource for teachers by modeling best practices for classroom instruction and helping teachers to continually develop their professional skills." The ad identified a number of duties and responsibilities, including the following:

• Coaching teachers, modeling lessons, and providing feedback and differentiated support for teachers.

• Developing and supporting a culture of reflective practice among teachers.

• Conducting planning meetings with teachers, reviewing classroom assignments, and creating plans for instruction.

• Working closely with the local instructional supervisor, principal, and assistant principal to assess teachers' needs and student data in order to plan relevant professional development.

• Facilitating workshops, courses, and study groups for teachers, supervisors, parents, and members of the instructional and guidance staffs.

The peer coach, as evidenced in the job description from New York, is an important person in the overall literacy effort in a middle or high school. However, most schools can afford only one peer coach, who then must attempt to support a huge number of teachers. For example, San Diego City Schools provide a peer coach for every school. This is an amazing resource for classroom teachers and their students. Unfortunately, in some schools, the single peer coach attempts to meet the needs of 150 teachers. Given that this is not a possible task, the peer coach often has to focus on specific teachers, such as teachers new to the profession, teachers who teach specific courses, or teachers who need instructional support. Again, this is an excellent resource for the teachers who get it, but far too many do not receive ongoing support, professional development, and mentoring.

We agree with Joyce and Showers (2002) that peer coaching needs to become a schoolwide structure. All teachers should be provided with the means of developing the skills required of a peer coach (Gottesman, 2000) as well as the time necessary to observe one another teach. Joyce and Showers (2002) note that when they work with entire school faculties, "all teachers and administrators agree to be members of peer coaching teams" (p. 88). They suggest that a number of agreements be made, including the following:

• Commitment to practice/use whatever change the faculty has agreed to implement.

• Assistance and support of each other in the change process, including shared planning of instructional objectives and development of materials and lessons.

• Collection of data, both on the implementation of their planned change and on student effects relevant to the school's identified target for student growth.

As you no doubt noticed in our rubric of quality indicators, we believe that the whole school should be involved in peer coaching. We expect to see teachers working together, collaborating on instructional ideas and lessons, observing one another teach, and engaging in conversations about their work. Some of these conversations are focused on student work, as discussed in the next section, and some of the conversations are focused on curriculum and instruction (Lapp, Fisher, Flood, & Frey, 2003).

It is important to note here that we are not recommending a schoolwide peer coaching initiative in place of a dedicated staff position. We support peer coaches, released teachers who organize and guide the professional development, but we know that they cannot accomplish the task alone. We also understand that teacher-to-teacher conversations can result in lasting changes and increased student achievement.

## Assessment and Student Progress

Why do we assess students? Think about this for a minute. What do we hope to get out of this use of time? Do we assess our students to find out what they do or do not know? Or do we assess and test students because this is part of

| AREA 5: LEADERSHIP AND SCHOOLWIDE SUPPORT 5. Is there a schoolwide emphasis on literacy, and does this focus develop teacher expertise? | | | | | |
|---|---|---|---|---|---|
| | **5** | **4** | **3** | **2** | **1** |
| 5.5. There is a schoolwide commitment to providing literacy assessments for the purpose of designing instruction and assessing student progress. | There is a system for creating common assessments, and all teachers review individual student performance data with their colleagues on a regular basis. These assessment conversations occur throughout the school year. | | Multiple assessments are used to determine student progress and needs; teachers volunteer to meet with one another to review student work. | | The assessments used in the school are limited to the state-mandated tests; teachers do not review assessment or test data with their peers. |

the "official" behavior of teachers? Or perhaps we assess students because state and federal laws require that we do so. Lapp, Fisher, Flood, and Cabello (2001) note that teachers assess students for at least four reasons:

• *Diagnosing individual student needs* (e.g., assessing developmental status, monitoring and communicating student progress, certifying competency, determining needs);

• *Informing instruction* (e.g., evaluating instruction, modifying instructional strategies, identifying instructional needs);

• *Evaluating programs;* and

• *Providing accountability information.* (p. 7)

Although each of these assessment purposes has a role in the overall work of a school, we will focus on the second purpose, to inform instruction. The link between assessment and instruction is an important one in the overall literacy initiative for middle and high schools.

Research evidence indicates that teachers can use student performance data to make instructional decisions and improvements (Fisher, Lapp, & Flood, 2005; Langer, Colton, & Goff, 2003). As Emily Calhoun (2004) notes, "In classrooms, schools, and districts, an ongoing system of data collection and use helps responsible parties make informed decisions" (p. 29). Valencia and Buly (2004) used student performance data to categorize struggling readers and to make instructional recommendations based on these reader profiles.

To make a difference, these assessments must be given routinely, not just at the end of the school year. In addition, groups of teachers must meet and discuss student performance data. These "assessment conversations," as Peter Johnston (2003) calls them, allow teachers to consider the needs of students and improve learning. However, these conversations can be constrained by our background knowledge and experience. Johnston notes:

> In theory, assessment is about gathering and interpreting data to inform action. In practice, data interpretations are constrained by our views of literacy and students, the assessment conversations that surround us, and the range of "actions" we can imagine. (p. 90)

Thankfully, there are several ways to encourage these "assessment conversations." For us, the ultimate form is consensus scoring. Consensus scoring differs in a number of key ways from other systems of examining student performance and assessment data. First, consensus scoring is not optional. Every teacher of a given subject is required to participate in the process—it becomes a schoolwide structure. This means that all teachers of Algebra I or U.S. History or 7th grade English for that matter, meet on a regular basis (every six to eight weeks) and examine assessment information.

The second main difference is that teachers create the assessments based on the standards they are teaching. This alignment is important because it allows teachers an opportunity to get to know the standards in new ways, and it provides teachers with an opportunity to consider the ways in which specific standards might be assessed.

The process of consensus scoring is fairly straightforward but requires significant leadership and investments in time. The first step is *unpacking the standards* (see Wiggins & McTighe, 1998). This requires that groups of teachers meet in course-alike groups to create pacing guides and curriculum maps. These pacing guides and curriculum maps allow teachers to plan lessons aligned with the state curriculum frameworks and standards. The pacing guide format from Hoover High School appears in Figure 5.4.

The second step is for teachers, again in their course-alike groups, to *develop common assessments*. Of course, these assessments must be aligned with standards; groups of teachers may need assistance in developing such assessment items. Fisher, Lapp, and Flood (2005) developed a checklist (see Figure 5.5 at the end of this chapter) that groups of teachers can use to create increasingly valid and reliable assessments. Creating these common

## FIGURE 5.4
### Curriculum Pacing Guide

Department:

Course:

| Standard | Unit of Study | Practices/Activities/Strategies | Assessments | Time Line |
|----------|---------------|--------------------------------|-------------|-----------|
| | | | | |

Vocabulary development (target and concept words)

Accommodations for Special Education and English Language Learners assessments reinforces an idea we presented earlier in this book—namely, that learning is language based. Invariably, all teachers will use reading, writing, speaking, listening, and viewing tasks to assess student progress.

The common assessments are not the only assessments teachers use. Individual teachers may use a range of assessments and tests to determine student progress, instructional needs, and grades. The common assessments can be used for these purposes or not; the decision is the teacher's. An important feature of the common assessments is that they provide teachers with performance data in real time, not at the end of the year when nothing can be done to improve student performance. (Fisher, Frey, Farnan, Fearn, & Peterson, 2004). As a side benefit, students who participate in common assessments are also receiving practice with various formats for assessment items, including practice demonstrating their knowledge in formats that resemble the accountability tests used in the state. Item-format practice is part of an overall test-improvement strategy that schools can use (Guthrie, 2002; Langer, 2001).

The third step in consensus scoring is to provide students with *high-quality curriculum and instruction*. As you know, this book has focused on high-quality curriculum and instruction. Although this issue may seem obvious, it is important to pause and reflect on it. We know that teachers matter, and what they *do* matters most. We believe that teachers come to work every day wanting to do what is best for their students. Focusing on high-quality curriculum and instruction as a part of the overall process allows groups of teachers to discuss their instructional repertoires and curriculum selections. Encouraging conversations about quality in curriculum and instruction adds process accountability to an accountability system otherwise solely focused on outcomes (Fisher, 2001a).

The fourth step requires that all teachers *collect assessment information* on all their students, on nearly the same day, using the common assessment tool that the group developed. The reason for this data collection is to ensure that every teacher has data to use during the final step of the process. This step also ensures that teachers are keeping to the pacing guide, so that some students don't end the year having missed major sections of knowledge. We have all heard the student complaint about U.S. History: "I don't know what happened after World War II; we never get that far in the class."

The final step in consensus scoring is the *assessment conversation*. Teachers, in their course-alike groups, meet to discuss results, implications, and needed changes in their practice. This is the heart of the process, in which teachers review aggregate student performance data. Their discussion may focus on areas of need within the group and how to meet those needs. Alternatively, their discussion may focus on revisions to the pacing guides or to the assessments themselves.

Let's consider two examples of consensus scoring in action. The first is from a 6th grade language arts class. The pacing guide focused on specific standards related to learning from expository texts. As a part of the consensus-scoring common assessment, students were asked to read a piece of informational text and to respond to the questions provided. The text the teachers selected focused on bullying at school, an issue for many middle school students. Here are two of the questions on the assessment:

> 3. According to the author, Kelsey was bullied because
>    (a) She was a witch.
>    (b) She didn't look and dress the same as the other girls.
>    (c) She was seeing a therapist.
>    (d) Her teachers didn't like her.
>
> 4. Which of the following is an opinion of the author?
>    (a) Thirty percent of students say that bullying is a problem.
>    (b) Kelsey should have changed schools.
>    (c) Adults should take bullying seriously.
>    (d) Bullying is not a serious problem in most schools.

The following table, the error analysis for these two questions, shows the number of students who chose each of the various answers. The bold numbers indicate how many students gave the correct answer.

| Questions | Answers | | | |
|-----------|-----|-----|-----|-----|
|           | A   | B   | C   | D   |
| 3         | 22  | **224** | 18 | 0 |
| 4         | 97  | 62  | **83** | 22 |

What do the data tell you? The 6th grade teachers were pleased, overall, with the performance of their students on Question 3, which focused on a fact that the author presented. They noted that a few students needed some reteaching on identifying facts. However, looking at the data for Question 4, they were concerned about the number of students who did not understand

the difference between an opinion and a fact (answer a) and a recommenda-
tion that they might have made but that was nowhere in the text (answer b).
The teachers' conversation then focused on what they should do with this
information. They wondered if they had "overtaught" the focus on facts. They
discussed some additional ways to teach students the difference between facts
and opinions and recommended books to one another that could be used to
reteach this concept. They also discussed the writing prompt that was given
as part of this consensus-scoring event and decided that they would focus
on students' writing using facts and opinions. At the end of the consensus-
scoring session with the whole group, teachers received their class data for
reflection and personal comparison to the whole group.

On the same day, a group of math teachers were meeting to discuss the
results of their common assessment. Here are two of the questions from
their assessment:

9. Solve the equation below using the order of operations.
   $(3 + 6) − 4 \, (2) =$
   (a) 10
   (b) 1
   (c) 17
   (d) 6

10. If a submarine is 20 feet below sea level and rises 6 feet, which is the correct equation and solution?
   (a) $20 + 6 = 26$
   (b) $−20 + −6 = −26$
   (c) $−20 + 6 = −14$
   (d) $20 + −6 = 14$

The following table shows the error analysis, with the bold numbers indicating how many students gave the correct answers.

| Questions | Answers | | | |
|---|---|---|---|---|
| | **A** | **B** | **C** | **D** |
| 9 | 51 | **122** | 10 | 10 |
| 10 | 42 | 21 | **111** | 19 |

In their conversations, the 8th grade math teachers expressed concern over
the number of students who still had not mastered the order of operations.
They discussed various reteaching ideas and decided to ask the administra-

tion for additional compensation for teachers who worked above and beyond their normal class loads to tutor individual students. They also noted the number of students who misunderstood the word problem. They discussed various ways to address this issue and decided to add daily "do now" activities at the start of the class. These "writing to learn" prompts would require that students solve word problems and explain their thinking in writing. They also decided that the next common assessment would require that students explain their thinking in writing so that the teachers would be able to "get inside their minds" and understand why they were making these mistakes.

As we have noted, consensus scoring is a process. It is a process that results in continuous improvement of student achievement. It also results in professional conversations that validate and extend each teacher's repertoire and expertise.

**✳ ✳ ✳ ✳ ✳ ✳ ✳**

To significantly improve adolescent literacy and content area achievement, we must move beyond individual teachers and isolated programs. This chapter has focused on the leadership demands and schoolwide structures that must be in place for radical changes to occur. Although individual teachers can become experts at developing literacy skills, it does, in fact, take the whole school to realize the dream of a literate citizenship.

---

**FIGURE 5.5**
**Checklist for Creating Assessments**

**All Items**

❑ Is this the most appropriate type of item to use for the intended learning outcomes?

❑ Does each item or task require students to demonstrate the performance described in the specific learning outcome it measures (relevance)?

❑ Does each item present a clear and definite task to be performed (clarity)?

❑ Is each item or task presented in simple, readable language and free from excessive verbiage (conciseness)?

❑ Does each item provide an appropriate challenge (ideal difficulty)?

*(continued)*

### FIGURE 5.5
### Checklist for Creating Assessments (Continued)

❑ Does each item have an answer that would be agreed upon by experts (correctness)?

❑ Is there a clear basis for awarding partial credit on items or tasks with multiple points (scoring rubric)?

❑ Is each item or task free from technical errors and irrelevant clues (technical soundness)?

❑ Is each test item free from cultural bias?

❑ Have the items been set aside for a time before reviewing them (or reviewed by a colleague)?

**Short-Answer Items**

❑ Can the items be answered with a number, symbol, word, or brief phrase?

❑ Has textbook language been avoided?

❑ Have the items been stated so that only one response is correct?

❑ Are the answer blanks equal in length (for fill-in responses)?

❑ Are the answer blanks (preferably one per item) at the end of the items, preferably after a question?

❑ Are the items free of clues (such as *a* or *an*)?

❑ Has the degree of precision been indicated for numerical answers?

❑ Have the units been indicated when numerical answers are expressed in units?

**Binary (True-False) and Multiple-Binary Items**

❑ Can each statement be clearly judged true or false with only one concept per statement?

❑ Have specific determiners (e.g., *usually, always*) been avoided?

❑ Have trivial statements been avoided?

❑ Have negative statements (especially double negatives) been avoided?

❑ Does a superficial analysis suggest a wrong answer?

❑ Are opinion statements attributed to some source?

❑ Are the true and false items approximately equal in length?

❑ Is there approximately an equal number of true and false items?

❑ Has a detectable pattern of answers (e.g., T, F, T, F) been avoided?

## FIGURE 5.5
### Checklist for Creating Assessments (Continued)

### Matching Items

❏ Is the material for the two lists homogeneous?

❏ Is the list of responses longer or shorter than the list of premises?

❏ Are the responses brief and on the right side?

❏ Have the responses been placed in alphabetical or numerical order?

❏ Do the directions indicate the basis for matching?

❏ Do the directions indicate how many times each response may be used?

❏ Are all of the matching items on the same page?

### Multiple-Choice Items

❏ Does each item stem present a meaningful problem?

❏ Is there too much information in the stem?

❏ Are the item stems free of irrelevant material?

❏ Are the item stems stated in positive terms (if possible)?

❏ If used, has negative wording been given special emphasis (e.g., capitalized)?

❏ Are the distractors brief and free of unnecessary words?

❏ Are the distractors similar in length and form to the answer?

❏ Is there only one correct or clearly best answer?

❏ Are the distractors based on specific misconceptions?

❏ Are the items free of clues that point to the answer?

❏ Are the distractors and answer presented in sensible (e.g., alphabetical, numerical) order?

❏ Have *all of the above* been avoided and have *none of the above* been used judiciously?

❏ If a stimulus is used, is it necessary for answering the item?

❏ If a stimulus is used, does it require use of skills sought to be assessed?

### Essay Items

❏ Are the questions designed to measure higher-level learning outcomes?

(*continued*)

## FIGURE 5.5
### Checklist for Creating Assessments (Continued)

❑ Does each question clearly indicate the response expected (including extensiveness)?

❑ Are students aware of the basis on which their answers will be evaluated?

❑ Are appropriate time limits provided for responding to the questions?

❑ Are students aware of the time limits and/or point values for each question?

❑ Are all students required to respond to the same questions?

### Performance Items

❑ Does the item focus on learning outcomes that require complex cognitive skills and student performances?

❑ Does the task represent both the content and skills that are central to learning outcomes?

❑ Does the item minimize dependence on skills that are irrelevant to the intended purpose of the assessment task?

❑ Does the task provide the necessary scaffolding for students to be able to understand the task and achieve the task?

❑ Do the directions clearly describe the task?

❑ Are students aware of the basis (expectations) on which their performances will be evaluated in terms of scoring rubrics?

### For the Assessment as a Whole

❑ Are the items of the same type grouped together on the test (or within sections or sets)?

❑ Are the items arranged from easy to more difficult within sections or the test as a whole?

❑ Are items numbered in sequence, indicating so if the test continues on subsequent pages?

❑ Are all answer spaces clearly indicated and is each answer space related to its corresponding item?

❑ Are the correct answers distributed in such a way that there is no detectable pattern?

❑ Is the test material well spaced, legible, and free of typos?

❑ Are there directions for each section of the test and the test as a whole?

❑ Are the directions clear and concise?

*Source:* Adapted by Fisher, Lapp, & Flood (2005) from Linn, R. L., & Gronlund, N. E. (2000). *Measurement and assessment in teaching* (8th ed.). Upper Saddle River, NJ: Merrill/Prentice Hall.

# Coda: A Student's Perspective on Improving Adolescent Literacy

A coda is a concluding musical section that is different from the main part of the selection. But a coda is more than that. A coda can also be the concluding part of a literary or dramatic work or something that serves to round out, conclude, or summarize something. It is with this intent that we offer the following coda.

Throughout this book we have referenced published works by people who study adolescent literacy. We have attempted to summarize our understanding of the research as well as our experiences in teaching adolescents to read, write, and think. However, Brozo (2002) reminds us that students are a critical stakeholder group and that the perspectives of students are important to consider in any initiative to improve schooling.

We decided to ask a student for his perspective on improving adolescent literacy. We selected a student who had significantly challenged the school system by his very attendance. Stephen Hinkle is a student who is autistic. He attended segregated classes in elementary school but was included in regular classes through middle and high school. He is currently a college student majoring in computer science. He has not read the professional literature about improving the achievement of secondary school students; he has not attended literacy conferences sponsored by the International Reading Association, the National Council of Teachers of English, the Association

for Supervision and Curriculum Development, or any other education organization; nor has he completed a credential program. We asked Stephen to
look back to his high school years and share his thoughts with us for
improving adolescent literacy achievement now that he is in college. He sent
us the following e-mail message:

1. Change the English curriculum to include an introduction to
college-level writing. A lot of the English curriculum is literature
reading, and I have heard that too many college kids end up failing
the English placement test when they get into college because of a
lack of writing skills.

2. I would suggest that students with reading difficulties have more
analysis to find out what their difficulties are. Some students have trouble with facts, stories, inference, and comprehension and they should
be taught how to correct such difficulties. Often standardized tests do
not test these skills adequately. In the silent reading classes, encourage
students to practice their skills that they are taught. Often what I see is
people either pretend to read or read something they like.

3. I support the ideas of incorporating literacy into other areas.
Students have to know how to read the information books. Students
need to be able to read different books and have a lot of things to
read. Students in today's world also need to understand the arts and
sciences, as this is what describes the world. I think that students
should have to explore the arts and sciences as a requirement to
graduate. Further on the arts and sciences part, I would suggest iso-
lating large blocks of time within the courses, for large hands-on
projects that cover multiple subject areas. Such ideas could include:

- Instead of reading a play, have students perform it. This way they
  will learn about the play and its characters, but also incorporate art,
  set design, lighting, sound, directing, oral communication, and more.
- Another example is to do a science project and do mathematical computations with the result. This way you implement science
  and math.
- Still another example is to do a project, in which someone
  makes a Web page about a historical topic, combining history
  with computer skills.

These are only a few examples, but such projects make the students learn a lot more and remember better than just studying and cramming for exams.

4. I would suggest that you incorporate a "Life Skills" curriculum, in which students prepare for living on their own. Students should be taught about money management, time management, cooking, good nutrition, the health care system, caring for themselves, hygiene, manners, ways to cooperate and share a space with others, survival skills, what to do in a disaster, sex education, teen pregnancy prevention, parenting, and other such issues of living on their own. They should be able to read about these things in their classes.

5. I would make sure the science curriculum includes teaching scientific principles, and that every child has a basic knowledge of science including life science, chemical science, and physical science. Students have to read and do labs to understand this.

6. I would make sure that every child gets PE and fitness education. Having children stay fit is important, especially with the obesity crisis in this country.

7. I think that the required curriculum should include computer skills like word processing, creating databases, spreadsheets, and graphics, using e-mail, browsing the Web, being aware of Internet safety, and having a basic knowledge of computer hardware. In the Internet safety portion, I would include an introduction to privacy, chat room safety, children's safety, copyright, network abuse, ethics, and ways to evaluate Internet accuracy. Students have to know how to read this stuff too.

8. I think that the electives offered should cover a wide range of areas that have the potential to help students down the road with their career, or stimulate interests for their major choice in college. I would consider offering courses in the following areas:

- Creative Arts
- Performing Arts
- Computer Technology
- Consumer Family Science
- Industrial Technology/Engineering

- Driver Education/Training
- Business Careers
- Student Government
- Yearbook
- Additional courses in core areas that cover non-traditional stuff such as science history, additional math areas, different types of English and writing, marine science, etc.

9. I would suggest having extracurricular activities that promote lifelong learning, fitness, and homework help, as well as opening kids to more of their world, and for kids to have a little bit of fun. Here are my ideas for such programs:

- After-school tutoring for many core subject areas
- Fitness and sports programs
- Interscholastic athletics
- Clubs
- Performing arts shows
- College prep enrichment
- SAT/ACT prep classes
- Library and computer lab open extended hours such as after school and on weekends for students to complete assignments

10. I would desegregate students with disabilities and make sure they have access to the entire general education curriculum. Students with disabilities need help from teachers to keep learning how to read and to "read between the lines" as my teachers told me. Additionally, I would have them do their life skills in a nonsegregated setting. I would also take steps to make sure they get to experience more extracurricular activities, and get standard diplomas.

Stephen's comments are specific and clear. This is not surprising given the recency of his experience in high school. The anecdotal information that Stephen provides is similar to the lessons that Harklau (2001) learned as she followed high school students from their senior year to college. Stephen's ideas also relate to current research ideas in adolescent literacy. As Moje (2002, pp. 224–225) notes,

The entire literacy field is missing a prime opportunity to learn not only about youth literacy but also from youth as they teach us about how complex literacy processes and practices develop and change in multiple contexts, times, and spaces. Until we include youth in general literacy theory (with the funding to assist our research and theorizing), we will continue to develop incomplete theories of literacy learning, development, and practice, and we will overlook a group of people with much to offer educational theory and the world.

We hope that this book has provided a glimpse inside the complex and intriguing world of adolescent literacy. It's a world that needs further exploration, for sure. But more important, it's a world we must navigate if we are to ensure that every student becomes a productive and contributing member of society.

# Appendix A: A Call to Action

## What We Know About Adolescent Literacy and Ways to Support Teachers in Meeting Students' Needs

### Purpose

The purpose of this document is to provide a research-based resource for media, policymakers, and teachers that acknowledges the complexities of reading as a developmental process and addresses the needs of secondary readers and their teachers.

### What Is Reading?

The National Council of Teachers of English (NCTE) Commission on Reading has produced a statement, "On Reading, Learning to Read, and Effective Reading Instruction," that synthesizes current research on reading. Reading is defined as a complex, purposeful, social, and cognitive process in which readers simultaneously use their knowledge of spoken and written language, their knowledge of the topic of the text, and their knowledge of their culture to construct meaning. Reading is not a technical skill acquired once and for all in the primary grades but rather a developmental process. A reader's competence continues to grow through engagement with various types of texts and wide reading for various purposes over a lifetime.

## What Is Unique About Adolescent Literacy?

In middle and high school, students encounter academic discourses and disciplinary concepts in such fields as science, mathematics, and the social sciences that require different reading approaches from those used with more familiar forms such as literary and personal narratives (Kucer, 2005). These new forms, purposes, and processing demands require that teachers show, demonstrate, and make visible to students how literacy operates within the academic disciplines (Keene & Zimmermann, 1997).

Adolescents are already reading in multiple ways, using literacy as a social and political endeavor in which they engage to make meaning and act upon their worlds. Their texts range from clothing logos to music to specialty magazines to Web sites to popular and classical literature. In the classroom it is important for teachers to recognize and value the multiple literacy resources students bring to the acquisition of school literacy.

In effective schools, classroom conversations about how, why, and what we read are important parts of the literacy curriculum (Applebee, 1996). In fact, discussion-based approaches to academic literacy content are strongly linked to student achievement (Applebee, Langer, Nystrand, & Gamoran, 2003). However, high-stakes testing, such as high school exit exams, is not only narrowing the content of the literacy curriculum but also constraining instructional approaches to reading (Amrein & Berliner, 2002; Madaus, 1998). Limited, "one right answer" or "main idea" models of reading run counter to recent research findings, which call for a richer, more engaged approach to literacy instruction (Campbell, Donahue, Reese, & Phillips, 1996; Taylor et al., 1999).

## What Current Research Is Showing Teachers

1. That literacy is a dynamic interaction of the social and cognitive realms, with textual understandings growing from students' knowledge of their worlds to knowledge of the external world (Langer, 2002). All students need to go beyond the study of discrete skills and strategies to understand how those skills and strategies are integrated with life experiences. Langer and colleagues (2003) found that literacy programs that successfully teach at-risk students emphasize connections between students' lives, prior knowledge, and texts, and emphasize student conversations to make those connections.

2. That the majority of inexperienced adolescent readers need opportunities and instructional support to read many and diverse types of texts in order to gain experience, build fluency, and develop a range as readers (Greenleaf, Schoenbach, Cziko, & Mueller, 2001; Kuhn & Stahl, 2000). Through extensive reading of a range of texts, supported by strategy lessons and discussions, readers become familiar with written language structures and text features, develop their vocabularies, and read for meaning more efficiently and effectively. Conversations about their reading that focus on the strategies they use and their language knowledge help adolescents build confidence in their reading and become better readers (Goodman & Marek, 1996).

3. That most adolescents do not need further instruction in phonics or decoding skills (Ivey & Baker, 2004). Research summarized in the National Reading Panel report noted that the benefits of phonics instruction are strongest in first grade, with diminished results for students in subsequent grades. Phonics instruction has not been seen to improve reading comprehension for older students (National Reading Panel, 2000). In cases where older students need help to construct meaning with text, instruction should be targeted and embedded in authentic reading experiences.

4. That utilizing a model of reading instruction focused on basic skills can lead to the mislabeling of some secondary readers as "struggling readers" and "non-readers" because they lack extensive reading experience, depend on different prior knowledge, and/or comprehend differently or in more complex ways. A large percentage of secondary readers who are so mislabeled are students of color and/or students from lower socioeconomic backgrounds. Abundant research suggests that the isolated skill instruction they receive may perpetuate low literacy achievement rather than improve their competence and engagement in complex reading tasks (Allington, 2001; Alvermann & Moore, 1991; Brown, 1991; Hiebert, 1991; Hull & Rose, 1989; Knapp & Turnbull, 1991; Sizer, 1992). In addition, prescriptive, skills-based reading instruction mislocates the problem as the students' failure to learn, rather than the institution's failure to teach reading as the complex mental and social activity it is (Greenleaf, Schoenbach, Cziko, & Mueller, 2001).

5. That effective literacy programs move students to deeper understandings of texts and increase their ability to generate ideas and knowledge for their own uses (Newmann, King, & Rigdon, 1997).

6. That assessment should focus on underlying knowledge in the larger curriculum and on strategies for thinking during literacy acts (Darling-Hammond & Falk, 1997; Langer, 2000; Smith, 1991). Likewise, preparation for assessment (from ongoing classroom measures to high-stakes tests) should focus on the critical components above.

## What Adolescent Readers Need

• Sustained experiences with diverse texts in a variety of genres and offering multiple perspectives on real-life experiences. Although many of these texts will be required by the curriculum, others should be self-selected and of high interest to the reader. Wide independent reading develops fluency, builds vocabulary and knowledge of text structures, and offers readers the experiences they need to read and construct meaning with more challenging texts. Text should be broadly viewed to include print, electronic, and visual media.

• Conversations and discussions regarding texts that are authentic, student initiated, and teacher facilitated. Such discussion should lead to diverse interpretations of a text that deepen the conversation.

• Experience in thinking critically about how they engage with texts:
  - When do I comprehend?
  - What do I do to understand a text?
  - When do I not understand a text?
  - What can I do when meaning breaks down?

• Experience in critical examination of texts that helps them to:
  - Recognize how texts are organized in various disciplines and genres.
  - Question and investigate various social, political, and historical content and purposes within texts.
  - Make connections between texts, and between texts and personal experiences to act on and react to the world.
  - Understand multiple meanings and richness of texts and layers of complexity.

## What Teachers of Adolescents Need

• Adequate and appropriate reading materials that tap students' diverse interests and represent a range of difficulty.

• Continued support and professional development that assist them to:

- Bridge between adolescents' rich literate backgrounds and school literacy.

- Teach literacy in their disciplines as an essential way of learning in their disciplines.

- Recognize when students are not making meaning with text and provide appropriate, strategic assistance to read course content effectively.

- Facilitate student-initiated conversations regarding texts that are authentic and relevant to real life experiences.

- Create environments that allow students to engage in critical examinations of texts as they dissect, deconstruct, and reconstruct in an effort to engage in meaning making and comprehension processes.

## Selected Resources for Teachers

Allen, J. (2000). *Yellow brick roads: Shared and guided paths to independent reading.* York, ME: Stenhouse.

Atwell, N. (1998). *In the middle* (2nd ed.). Portsmouth, NH: Heinemann.

Beers, K. (2003). *When kids can't read: What teachers can do.* Portsmouth, NH: Heinemann.

Lenski, S., Wham, M. A., & Johns, J. (2003). *Reading and learning strategies middle grades through high school.* Dubuque, IA: Kendall/Hunt.

Robb, L. (2000). *Teaching reading in middle school.* New York: Scholastic.

Schoenbach, R., Greenleaf, C., Cziko, C., & Hurwitz, L. (1999). *Reading for understanding: A guide to improving reading in middle and high school classrooms.* San Francisco: Jossey-Bass.

Smith, M., & Wilhelm, J. (2002). *"Reading don't fix no chevy's": Literacy in the lives of young men.* Portsmouth, NH: Heinemann.

Tovani, C. (2000). *I read it but I don't get it.* York, ME: Stenhouse.

Wilhelm, J., Baker, T., & Dube, J. (2001). *Strategic reading: Guiding students to lifelong literacy.* Portsmouth, NH: Heineman.

*Source:* From "A Call to Action: What We Know About Adolescent Literacy and Ways to Support Teachers in Meeting Students' Needs" by National Council of Teachers of English Commission on Reading, May 2004. Position statement available: www.ncte.org/about/over/positions/category/read/118622.htm. Reprinted with permission.

# Appendix B: Adolescent Literacy

## Adolescents Deserve More

Carol Minnick Santa, President,
International Reading Association

I want to thank the members of the International Reading Association's Commission on Adolescent Literacy (CAL) for the development of this position paper, which was approved by the Association's Board of Directors in May 1999. Ironically, the Board approved this statement in the aftermath of the shattering violence at Columbine High School in Colorado—a vivid and horrible testimony to the ever-deepening crises in adolescent literacy. If only these young men had been touched by a book or a teacher, or had felt more connected with their school, perhaps none of this would have happened. As teachers and parents, we have to do things differently.

This position statement is a start. We must begin with a clear message about what adolescents deserve. Adolescents are being shortchanged. No one is giving adolescent literacy much press. It is certainly not a hot topic in educational policy or a priority in schools. In the United States, most Title I budgets are allocated for early intervention—little is left over for the struggling adolescent reader. Even if all children do learn to read by Grade 3, the literacy needs of the adolescent reader are far different from those of primary-grade children. Many people don't recognize reading development as a continuum. Moreover, schools have worked hard to reduce class size for children in grades K–3, while at the same time we have watched a steady increase in class size as children progress through school. Reading specialists have become history in too many middle and high schools.

I speak for the Association's Board of Directors as we unanimously endorse the powerful messages in this document. We hope it will provide you with a tool for becoming a stronger advocate for the adolescents in your neighborhood school, your community, your state or province, and your country.

## A Day in the Literacy Lives of Nick and Kristy Araujo

"Hey, Nick, wake up!" Nick Araujo felt his friend Adam's punch in the arm, jolting him out of his daydream in fourth-period English at Polytechnic High. Mr. Potter, his teacher, had assigned Charles Dickens's *A Tale of Two Cities,* a really ancient book that Nick's dad said he had to read years ago. Today they were supposed to take an essay test on the book. They never talked about what they read, and, anyway, Nick was preoccupied with thoughts about the new virtual bass fishing game he'd read about in his *North American Fisherman* magazine.

Fortunately, the video he'd watched of *A Tale of Two Cities* got him through the essay test ordeal, then it was on to psychology class. Mr. Jackson was great. He knew how to make any topic interesting, and his class seemed more like a television talk show than school. Nick struggled with reading, but he loved watching movies, and he was able to use his vast knowledge of cinema in this class. Yesterday they had talked about a film of people meeting on the Internet, and today's discussion was about why some people create false identities in Internet chat rooms.

As the final bell rang, Nick headed out to his small truck in the parking lot. He was off to the gym to lift some weights. At least he didn't have to work today; there was lots of time for the assignment from his history class. That teacher just dumped work on them without any idea of what she wanted. Nick was supposed to write a five-paragraph essay about a famous person. That was all the instruction Mrs. Nathan provided. Maybe his hotshot sister, Kristy, could help.

"No, Nick," Kristy said, when he got home. "I have to practice my serves for volleyball, and I have to study for a science test. I hate science. All we do is read the book, and then he gives us a test. I don't have time to do your homework, too!"

"There goes Kristy again," Nick thought. It was hard to be the brother of a straight-A seventh grader who was a star athlete too. Nick plunked down on the couch and turned on the *Legend of Zelda* video game. Off into the world of Hyrule. "Hey, Kristy, I need to know what *dispel* means for this game."

"I don't know. Figure it out or go look it up in the dictionary yourself!"

Nick looked it up, then passed into the Zora domain.

"Mom, what famous person should I do my essay on?"

"You like hunting, Nick. How about Daniel Boone or Davy Crockett? They're famous people who hunted."

Nick headed into the family room, where the computer was, to search the Internet for some information on famous hunters. Of course Kristy was hogging the computer again. She was probably in a chat room with her friends or writing in her secret diary. Or she was playing that geography game again. "Kristy's idea of fun looks like work to me," Nick thought.

"Hey, Kristy, I thought you had to study. It's my turn."

Kristy bounced out of the room, grabbing a copy of *Chicken Soup for the Teenage Soul*. Time for a quick story before tackling her boring science assignment.

She read the section of her textbook on mitosis and meiosis and dutifully outlined it. Mr. Taylor didn't care if they understood it; they only needed to memorize key parts for the test. She finished quickly, then went outside and hit volleyballs against a wall.

Meanwhile, Nick printed out a biography on Davy Crockett and headed into the kitchen to help his mom with a quick microwave dinner.

After dinner, Kristy went back on the computer to begin her assignment for language arts class. She loved to search the Internet. They had read Mildred D. Taylor's *Roll of Thunder, Hear My Cry,* and her assignment was to research events during the Great Depression that might have affected Cassie's life. There was sure to be a lively discussion tomorrow in class, and Kristy wanted to be prepared. She enjoyed Mrs. Mangrum's class.

Nick disappeared upstairs to compose his essay while talking to his girl-friend, Jennifer, on the phone. Kristy finished her work for language arts class and settled down to watch her favorite series on television. Then it was time for bed and a few minutes of reading *Teen People* magazine.

Nick fell asleep, sprawled on his bed with his nearly completed essay scattered on his bedroom floor.

This fictional account of Nick and Kristy's day illustrates how adolescents read and write amid conditions they and their families, friends, schools, and society establish. To be sure, Kristy and Nick's day only hints at the actual literacy practices of the more than 20,000,000 students currently enrolled in U.S. middle and high schools. Adolescents use print—and learn how to use print—in countless ways.

Despite the prevalence of literacy in adolescents' lives, educational policies, school curricula, and the public currently are neglecting [this crucial skill]. For instance, state and federal funding for middle and high school reading programs in the United States has decreased. Fewer and fewer schools are able to hire reading specialists who work with individual students and help teachers of all subjects be more effective teachers of reading. The limited number of reading education courses required for preservice middle and high school teachers often does not sufficiently prepare them to respond to the escalating needs of adolescent learners.

This position statement developed by the International Reading Association Commission on Adolescent Literacy (CAL) calls for the literacy of adolescents to be addressed directly and effectively. We begin by responding to questions that bring into the open some common misconceptions.

## Questions and Answers About Adolescent Literacy

### Shouldn't adolescents already be literate?

As the story of Nick and Kristy's day indicates, adolescents generally have learned a great deal about reading and writing, but they have not learned all they need. For instance, the 1998 Reading Report Card produced by the National Assessment of Educational Progress (NAEP) showed that a majority of U.S. adolescents (approximately 60 percent) can comprehend specific factual information. Yet few have gone beyond the basics to advanced reading and writing. Fewer than five percent of the adolescents NAEP assessed could extend or elaborate the meanings of the materials they read. The NAEP writing assessments have indicated that few adolescents could write effective pieces with sufficient details to support main points.

Adolescents entering the adult world in the 21st century will read and write more than at any other time in human history. They will need advanced levels of literacy to perform their jobs, run their households, act as citizens, and conduct their personal lives. They will need literacy to cope with the flood of information they will find everywhere they turn. They will need literacy to feed their imaginations so they can create the world of the future. In a complex and sometimes even dangerous world, their ability to read will be crucial. Continual instruction beyond the early grades is needed.

### Couldn't the problem be solved by preventing reading difficulties early on?

Reading success in the early grades certainly pays off later, but early achievement is not the end of the story. Just as children pass through stages of turning over, sitting up, crawling, walking, and running as they develop control of their bodies, there are developmental stages of reading and writing. During the preschool and primary school years, children learn how written language can be used for purposes such as telling stories and recording facts, how print is arranged on a page, and how letters and sounds combine to form words. These are major accomplishments, but they are only the first steps of growth into full literacy.

When all goes well, upper grade youth increase their reading fluency and adjust their reading speed according to their reasons for reading. They discern the characteristics of different types of fiction and nonfiction materials. They refine their tastes in reading and their responses to literature. Middle and high school students build on the literacy strategies they learned in the early grades to make sense of abstract, complex subjects far removed from their personal experiences. For Nick, Kristy, and other adolescents, the microscopic realm explained in a science book and the French Revolution depicted in *A Tale of Two Cities* can be strange worlds described in alien words.

The need to guide adolescents to advanced stages of literacy is not the result of any teaching or learning failure in the preschool or primary years; it is a necessary part of normal reading development. Guidance is needed so that reading and writing develop along with adolescents' ever increasing oral language, thinking ability, and knowledge of the world.

Even with the best instruction early on, differences magnify as students develop from year to year. Today's adolescents enter school speaking many different languages and coming from many different backgrounds and experiences, so their academic progress differs substantially. Some teens need special instruction to comprehend basic ideas in print. Others need extensive opportunities with comfortable materials so they learn to read smoothly and easily. And almost all students need to be supported as they learn unfamiliar vocabulary, manage new reading and writing styles, extend positive attitudes toward literacy, and independently apply complex learning strategies to print.

## Why isn't appropriate literacy instruction already being provided to adolescents?

Exemplary programs of adolescent literacy instruction certainly exist, but they are the exception because upper grade goals often compete with reading development. Elementary schools traditionally emphasize mathematics and literacy instruction, but middle and secondary schools generally shift attention to other matters.

Middle school programs often emphasize an expanded range of student needs: physical, emotional, and social, as well as academic. Although literacy growth might be recognized as important, many schools do not include reading instruction in the curriculum for all students. Language arts teachers often have sole responsibility for guiding students' reading growth while still being held accountable for covering a literature program, teaching grammar, offering personal advisory programs, and so on.

High school teachers often feel a great responsibility to impart knowledge about subjects such as science or history in which they are expert. This focus on subject matter is supported by the typical organization of high schools with the faculty assigned to separate departments and the day divided among separate subjects. Many teachers come to believe that teaching students how to effectively read and write is not their responsibility. Without intending to do so, they might send subtle messages that adolescents' continued growth in reading and writing is incidental.

## So is there a solution?

There are no easy answers or quick fixes. Adolescents deserve nothing less than a comprehensive effort to support their continued development as readers and writers. A productive first step is for all involved in the lives of adolescents to commit themselves to definite programs of literacy growth. The CAL recommends the following principles as touchstones for such programs.

## What Adolescents Deserve: Principles for Supporting Adolescents' Literacy Growth

### 1. Adolescents deserve access to a wide variety of reading material that they can and want to read.

The account of Kristy and Nick's day shows adolescents reading inside- and outside-of-school print such as textbooks, paperbacks, magazines, and Web sites. Yet national assessments provoke concern about the amount of such reading among adolescents. For instance, the 1996 NAEP findings indicate that about one quarter of the tested adolescents reported daily reading of five or fewer pages in school and for homework. As students grow older, the amount of time they read for fun declines. About one half of the tested nine-year-old students reported reading for fun on a daily basis, whereas only about one quarter of the 17-year-old students reported doing so. Literacy research and professional judgment support at least four reasons for providing adolescents access to inside- and outside-of-school reading materials they can and want to read.

- *Time spent reading is related to reading success.* If students devote some time every day reading connected text, their word knowledge, fluency, and comprehension tend to increase. Reading continuously for a brief part of each day is a small investment for a large return.
- *Time spent reading is associated with attitudes toward additional reading.* Students who habitually read in the present tend to seek out new materials in the future. These students are on the way to lifelong reading.
- *Time spent reading is tied to knowledge of the world.* Combining materials such as textbooks, library books, paperbacks, magazines, and Web sites provides full accounts of phenomena, new vocabulary, and up-to-date information. These materials permit readers to expand and strengthen their grasp of the world.
- *Reading is a worthwhile life experience.* Readers can find comfort and delight in print. Vicariously stepping into text worlds can nourish teens' emotions and psyches as well as their intellects.

Providing opportunities to achieve the outcomes just listed is accomplished through a network of educators, librarians, parents, community members, peers, policy makers, technology providers, and publishers. These groups affect middle and high school students' access to wide reading by shaping the following elements:

- *Time.* An often overlooked—yet essential—component of access to reading is the time available for it. Adolescents deserve specific opportunities to schedule reading into their days.

- *Choice.* Choosing their own reading materials is important to adolescents who are seeking independence. All adolescents, and especially those who struggle with reading, deserve opportunities to select age-appropriate materials they can manage and topics and genres they prefer. Adolescents deserve classroom, school, and public libraries that offer reading materials tied to popular television and movie productions; magazines about specific interests such as sports, music, or cultural backgrounds; and books by favorite authors. They deserve book clubs, class sets of paperbacks, and personal subscriptions to magazines.

- *Support.* Time and choice mean little if there is no support. Support includes actions such as bringing books to the classroom, arousing interest in them, orally reading selections, and fostering student-to-student and student-to-adult conversations about what is read. Adolescents deserve these supports so they will identify themselves as readers and take advantage of the times and choices that are offered.

## 2. Adolescents deserve instruction that builds both the skill and desire to read increasingly complex materials.

Kristy and Nick Araujo tackled their assignments with a few basic reading and writing strategies. Outlining text passages and looking up an unfamiliar word like *dispel* in the dictionary are some of strategies Nick and Kristy used in their studies. However, these teens will need to expand their strategies to handle increasingly complex material now and in the future. In addition, Nick's history as a struggling reader indicates he will need extra help if he is to grasp future concepts successfully. Adolescents need well-developed repertoires of reading comprehension and study strategies such as the following:

- Questioning themselves about what they read;
- Synthesizing information from various sources;
- Identifying, understanding, and remembering key vocabulary;

- Recognizing how a text is organized and using that organization as a tool for learning;
- Organizing information in notes;
- Interpreting diverse symbol systems in subjects such as biology and algebra;
- Searching the Internet for information;
- Judging their own understanding; and
- Evaluating authors' ideas and perspectives.

Many teaching practices are available for supporting adolescent learners as they apply strategies to complex texts. For example, teachers who introduce some of the technical vocabulary students will encounter in a chapter help reduce comprehension problems, and students help themselves by independently previewing passages and discerning the meanings of unfamiliar words. Study guide questions and statements that prompt students from literal understandings to higher order ones also foster comprehension. When teachers inform students while the guides are being phased out, adolescents can appropriate for themselves the thinking strategies the guides stimulated.

Middle and secondary schools where reading specialists work with content area teachers in the core areas of science, mathematics, English, and social studies show great promise. For example, a reading specialist's work with a social studies teacher to map ideas during a unit on the Aztec, Inca, and Mayan cultures can become the basis for teaching students to map ideas as an independent study strategy. The CAL recommends that content area teachers and reading specialists work together to effectively support adolescents' development of advanced reading strategies.

Developing students' advanced reading skills is insufficient if adolescents choose not to read. Unfortunately, students' attitudes toward reading tend to decline as they advance into the middle grades, with a particularly disturbing impact on struggling readers like Nick. Attitudes toward reading contribute to reading achievement.

Caring teachers who act on adolescents' interests and who design meaningful inquiry projects address motivational needs. For example, Kristy was excited about independently researching events of the Great Depression that affected Cassie's life in *Roll of Thunder, Hear My Cry*. Based on her experiences in this class, Kristy knew she would have an attentive audience for discussing her research and a considerate teacher supporting and evaluating her demonstration of knowledge. Mrs. Mangrum regularly fostered discussions of multicultural literature, and she expressed sincere interest in her students' wide ranging cultural and ethnic differences, learning styles, and needs for respect and security. In addition to having the whole class read and talk about one particular novel, Mrs. Mangrum provided students access to various books for self-selected reading on their own. She gleaned books from her own classroom collection, students' recommendations, and a close working relationship with her school librarian. Adolescents deserve classrooms like Mrs. Mangrum's that knowingly promote the desire to read.

### 3. Adolescents deserve assessment that shows them their strengths as well as their needs and that guides their teachers to design instruction that will best help them grow as readers.

National-level mandates on education such as Goals 2000 and the reauthorization of the Elementary and Secondary Education Act in the United States require that states develop standards for instruction and assess student achievement of the standards. In some states these measures are being used to determine the type of diploma students receive and whether or not students will even graduate. Although state assessments are useful in monitoring the achievement of standards, they rarely indicate specific teaching-learning experiences that foster literacy development.

Adolescents deserve classroom assessments that bridge the gap between what they know and are able to do and relevant curriculum standards; they deserve assessments that map a path toward continued literacy growth. For instance, when Nick began writing his essay about a famous person, he did not seem clear about the expected standards. He probably would have benefited from understanding how writing this particular essay connected with the world beyond the classroom. He could have used lessons on how to accomplish expectations. He might have benefited from examining papers that reflected the expected standards. And he could have profited from a rubric or scoring guide that clearly articulated the standards for evaluation.

Conferring with his teacher and classmates about how his efforts fit curriculum standards also might have promoted Nick's writing. During such conferences he would have opportunities to assess his own writing, set specific goals, and decide on strategies for achieving his goals. Further, Nick would benefit from maintaining a record of his efforts in something like a portfolio to help gauge his reading and writing growth and plan appropriate actions. Emphasizing relevance and self-improvement in classroom assessment encourages adolescents to invest themselves in learning. It helps them understand how to control the rate and quality of their own literacy growth.

Effective assessments are crucial for students who come from environments that differ from Kristy and Nick's. Using tests simply to determine which students will graduate or which type of diploma students will receive especially disadvantages adolescents from homes where English is not the first language or where poverty endures. It wrongs those most in need of enriched educational opportunities.

In sum, the CAL believes that adolescents deserve classroom assessments that

- Are regular extensions of instruction;
- Provide usable feedback based on clear, attainable, and worthwhile standards;
- Exemplify quality performances illustrating the standards; and
- Position students as partners with teachers evaluating progress and setting goals.

### 4. Adolescents deserve expert teachers who model and provide explicit instruction in reading comprehension and study strategies across the curriculum.

Like masters with apprentices, expert teachers immerse students in a discipline and teach them how to control it. Expert teachers engage students with a novel such as *Roll of Thunder, Hear My Cry* in Kristy's language arts class or a topic such as the presentation of self in Nick's psychology class. Then they teach reading, writing, and thinking strategies that enable students to explore and learn about subject matter. Reading and subject matter teachers often collaborate to provide such instruction.

If Kristy's teacher, Mrs. Mangrum, were teaching self-questioning as a strategy, she might first take a chapter of *Roll of Thunder, Hear My Cry* and model queries such as "What became clear to me?" and "I wonder why Cassie didn't complain to her teacher about the school bus driver running them off the road." Mrs. Mangrum would explain how she arrived at answers to her questions, thinking through the process aloud. She would explicitly demonstrate how to ask and answer productive questions during this stage of instruction.

Next Mrs. Mangrum and Kristy's class might produce questions and answers collectively, again thinking aloud. At first they might stay with the chapter Mrs. Mangrum began with, or they might move to another. Together the students and teacher would explain and comment on what they were doing. Additionally, Mrs. Mangrum might provide written guides for students to question themselves, exploring and experimenting with the strategy on their own. She also might design small group assignments that encourage students to reflect on self-questioning, sharing how they used it and difficulties they overcame.

Eventually Mrs. Mangrum would expect Kristy and her classmates to apply self-questioning on their own. She would remind students to question themselves while reading other novels and passages later in the year. Throughout this cycle of instruction, she would have students assess how well they were accomplishing the strategy. Research on expert teachers has produced an image of decision makers effectively orchestrating classroom life. Expert teachers help students get to the next level of strategy development by addressing meaningful topics, making visible certain strategies, then gradually releasing responsibility for the strategies to the learners. Adolescents deserve such instruction in all their classes.

## 5. Adolescents deserve reading specialists who assist individual students having difficulty learning how to read.

In the early 1900s standardized tests in the United States revealed large numbers of adolescents reading well below expectations. This finding sparked many educators and members of the public to develop programs for adolescents that included remedial instruction in reading classes and modified instruction in regular subject-matter classes. Federally funded programs to compensate for the effects of poverty on achievement later were instituted for reading, writing, and mathematics instruction.

National-level data continue highlighting the presence of adolescents like Nick with reading needs. For instance, 13 percent of fall 1989 first-year higher education students in the United States were enrolled in courses devoted specifically to remedial reading. The high school dropout rate, which is related to literacy difficulties, was 11 percent in 1993. Race, ethnicity, and economic status continue to be strongly associated with reading achievement. Although the number of secondary schools that assist adolescents who struggle with reading is declining, most schools still provide programs. These include widely varying provisions such as special education classes, after school tutoring, and content reading integration.

Reading difficulties do not occur in a vacuum. Adolescents' personal identities, academic achievement, and future aspirations mix with ongoing difficulties with reading. Because literacy promises to enhance individuals as well as society, adolescents struggling with reading deserve assistance by professionals specially prepared in reading. The CAL recommends services that include the following:

• Providing tutorial reading instruction that is part of a comprehensive program connected with subject matter teachers, parents, and the community;

• Structuring challenging, relevant situations in special reading classes and in subject matter classrooms where students succeed and become self-sufficient learners;

• Assessing students' reading and writing—and enabling students to assess their own reading and writing—to plan instruction, foster individuals' control of their literacy, and immediately support learners when progress diminishes;

• Teaching vocabulary, fluency, comprehension, and study strategies tailored to individuals' competencies;

• Relating literacy practices to life management issues such as exploring careers, examining individuals' roles in society, setting goals, managing time and stress, and resolving conflicts; and

• Offering reading programs that recognize potentially limiting forces such as work schedules, family responsibilities, and peer pressures.

### 6. Adolescents deserve teachers who understand the complexities of individual adolescent readers, respect their differences, and respond to their characteristics.

Adolescents demonstrate substantial differences. In the Araujo family, Nick's interests in film and the outdoors differed from Kristy's preferences for athletics and teen culture. Nick tended to struggle with and avoid school-based reading and writing tasks; Kristy generally excelled with and enthusiastically approached them.

Viewing members of one family in relation to another calls attention to additional differences. Factors such as family heritage, language, and social and economic position contribute to the variation that students regularly display during reading and writing activities.

Differences also are apparent when individuals are considered one at a time. Nick often was preoccupied in one class, English, but highly engaged in another, psychology. Kristy hated how her science teacher conducted class but enjoyed language arts. Nick and Kristy probably acted slightly differently from day to day in all their classes depending on what was happening in their personal worlds.

Adolescents deserve classrooms that respect individuals' differences. To promote respect, teachers encourage the exchange of ideas among individuals. They regularly set up paired, small group, and whole class arrangements so that everyone can have his or her voice heard. Believing that everyone has something to offer, they organize instruction so students of diverse backgrounds share their insights into course topics. One of the reasons Kristy eagerly researched the Great Depression was that she anticipated a productive discussion the next day.

Respectful classrooms are safe enough for students to take risks when expressing themselves publicly. No rudeness, put-downs, or ugly remarks are allowed. Learners address others courteously and expect courteous treatment in turn. They disagree without being disagreeable, contesting others' ideas without personal insults.

Respectful classrooms also display positive expectations. Teachers believe that students who are taught appropriately can meet rigorous standards. They acknowledge conditions outside of class that might interfere with learning, but they inspire teens to be resilient and take charge of their lives. Learning failures are unacceptable.

Along with respect, individual adolescents deserve teachers who respond to their characteristics. Responsive teachers address the mandated curriculum while engaging students in self-expression. To illustrate, Nick's five-paragraph report on a famous person could be extended several ways. Nick could inquire into Davy Crockett through interviews, library materials, and textbooks as well as through the Internet. He could enrich his investigation by examining legendary aspects of Crockett or he could look at Crockett's role as an icon of individualism. Nick could supplement his essay by representing Crockett through a poem, poster, readers theatre, or skit. Teachers often limit such choices to manageable options, but they offer choices and supports for accomplishing them.

In sum, adolescents deserve more than a centralized, one-size-fits-all approach to literacy. They deserve teachers who establish productive conditions for learning; move into individuals' worlds with respect, choice, and support; and move out to allow growth.

## 7. Adolescents deserve homes, communities, and a nation that will support their efforts to achieve advanced levels of literacy and provide the support necessary for them to succeed.

For adolescents, growing in literacy means being continually stretched. Because of this, adolescents deserve all the support they can get, not only from school but from their families, communities, and the nation.

Parents play an important role. They help adolescents extend and consolidate their literacy by engaging them in discussions about what they read, responding sincerely to the ideas they write, and making printed materials available. Parents become partners with educators in supporting their adolescents' growth.

Members of the local community often are partners with adolescents. Libraries, religious groups, and after school programs are centers for community workers and volunteers to assist adolescents with homework, tutor individuals with learning difficulties, and initiate book discussion groups. Businesses become partners with schools by providing mentors and role models as well as funds for buying books and recognizing achievements.

Adolescents preparing for the 21st century deserve new forms of collaboration among educators. Community colleges, technical schools, and universities can offer input and assistance. Professional organizations working together and exploring relationships among reading, writing, and learning may lead to new educational directions. The educational community can demonstrate that adolescent literacy is important.

The many dimensions of adolescent literacy are addressed best in school reform and restructuring that place the growth of students at the center of every activity. Environments of high expectations, inquiry, and decision making encourage students to refine the reading and writing abilities they have and take the risks necessary to grow. Adolescents deserve new perspectives on what it means to know a subject and to display that knowledge. Surface changes to schools involving scheduling and required courses are not enough to fully support adolescents' advanced reading and writing.

Finally, the CAL believes that the literacy achievement of adolescents cannot grow to new levels without changes in governmental policy. Emphasizing the achievement of early readers has not produced adolescents who read and write at high levels of proficiency. Adolescents deserve increased levels of governmental support. This includes appropriate funding for intervention services in the upper grades, the point in most comparisons at which children in the United States perform less well. School libraries can be the center of efforts to encourage wide reading, but for decades they have seen a steady decline in funding. Governmental support also involves exerting leadership to mobilize initiatives among parents and local communities.

The government can support ongoing staff development for helping students grow in literacy as they grow in content knowledge. Furthermore, government can support literacy research concentrating on the upper grades where literacy proficiencies are less well understood than those at the lower grades.

## A Commitment to Growth

Public and educational attention long has been focused on the beginnings of literacy, planting seedlings and making sure that they take root. But without careful cultivation and nurturing, seedlings may wither and their growth becomes stunted. We, as members of the International Reading Association Commission on Adolescent Literacy, urge policy makers, administrators, business people, community members, parents, and educators to commit themselves to supporting adolescents' literacy in the ways presented in this position statement. Adolescents deserve enhanced opportunities to grow into healthy, strong, and independent readers and writers.

## Suggested Readings
***Shouldn't adolescents already be literate?***

Berliner, D. C., & Biddle, B. J. (1995). *The manufactured crisis: Myths, fraud, and attacks on America's public schools.* Reading, MA: Addison-Wesley.

Campbell, J. R., Voelkl, K. E., & Donahue, P. L. (1998). *Report in brief: NAEP 1996 trends in academic progress* (Publication No. 98-530). Washington, DC: National Center for Education Statistics.

Graham, P. A. (1981). Literacy: A goal for secondary schools. *Daedalus, 110*(3), 119–134.

Kibby, M. W. (1995). *Student literacy: Myths and realities.* Bloomington, IN: Phi Delta Kappa Educational Foundation.

National Assessment of Educational Progress. (1999). *NAEP 1998 reading report card for the nation and the states* [Online]. Available: http://www.ed.gov/NCES/NAEP.

### Couldn't the problem be solved by preventing reading difficulties early on?

Chall, J. S. (1983). *Stages of reading development.* New York: McGraw-Hill.

Gee, T. C., & Rakow, S. J. (1991). Content reading education: What methods do teachers prefer? *NASSP Bulletin, 75,* 104–110.

Schumm, J. S., Vaughn, S., & Saumell, L. (1992). What teachers do when the textbook is tough: Students speak out. *Journal of Reading Behavior, 24,* 481–503.

Smith, F. R., & Feathers, K. M. (1983). The role of reading in content classrooms: Assumption vs. reality. *Journal of Reading, 27,* 262–267.

U.S. Department of Education, National Center for Education Statistics. (1997). *The condition of education, 1997* (NCES 97-388). Washington, DC: U.S. Government Printing Office.

Wells, M. C. (1995). *Literacies lost: When students move from a progressive middle school to a traditional high school.* New York: Teachers College Press.

### Why isn't appropriate literacy instruction already being provided to adolescents?

Alvermann, D., & Moore, D. (1991). Secondary school reading. In R. Barr, M. L. Kamil, P. Mosenthal, & P. D. Pearson (Eds.), *Handbook of reading research* (Vol. II, pp. 951–983). White Plains, NY: Longman.

O'Brien, D., Stewart, R., & Moje, E. B. (1995). Why content literacy is difficult to infuse into the secondary school: Complexities of curriculum, pedagogy, and school culture. *Reading Research Quarterly, 30,* 442–463.

Oldfather, P., & Thomas, S. (1998). What does it mean when high school teachers participate in collaborative research with students on literacy motivations? *Teachers College Record, 99,* 647–691.

Perrone, V., & Traver, R. (1996). Secondary education. In J. Sikula, T. J. Buttery, & E. Guyton (Eds.), *Handbook of research on teacher education* (2nd ed., pp. 392–409). New York: Macmillan.

Romine, B. G. C., McKenna, M. C., & Robinson, R. D. (1996). Reading coursework requirements for middle and high school content area teachers: A U.S. survey. *Journal of Adolescent & Adult Literacy, 40,* 194–198.

Vacca, R. (1998). Let's not marginalize adolescent literacy. *Journal of Adolescent & Adult Literacy, 41,* 604–609.

### Adolescents deserve access to a wide variety of reading material that they can and want to read.

Anderson, R. C., Wilson, P. T., & Fielding, L. G. (1988). Growth in reading and how children spend their time outside of school. *Reading Research Quarterly, 23,* 285–303.

Campbell, J. R., Voelkl, K. E., & Donahue, P. L. (1998). *Report in brief: NAEP 1996 trends in academic progress* (Publication No. 98-530). Washington, DC: National Center for Education Statistics.

Cone, J. K. (1994). Appearing acts: Creating readers in a high school English class. *Harvard Educational Review, 64,* 450–473.

Fielding, L., & Roller, C. (1992). Making difficult books accessible and easy books acceptable. *The Reading Teacher, 45,* 678–687.

Fielding, L. G. (1994). Independent reading. In A. Purves (Ed.), *Encyclopedia of English studies and language arts* (Vol. I, p. 613). New York: Scholastic/National Council of Teachers of English.

Ivey, G. (1998). Discovering readers in the middle level school: A few helpful clues. *NASSP Bulletin, 82*(600), 48–56.

Nell, V. (1988). *Lost in a book: The psychology of reading for pleasure.* New Haven, CT: Yale University Press.

Rosenblatt, L. M. (1978). *The reader, the text, the poem: The transactional theory of the literary work.* Carbondale, IL: Southern Illinois University Press.

Worthy, J., Moorman, M., & Turner, M. (1999). What Johnny likes to read is hard to find in school. *Reading Research Quarterly, 34,* 12–53.

### Adolescents deserve instruction that builds both the skill and desire to read increasingly complex materials.

Bean, T. W., Valerio, P. C., & Stevens, L. (1999). Content area literacy instruction. In L. B. Gambrell, & L. M. Morrow (Eds.), *Best practices in literacy instruction* (pp. 175–192). New York: Guilford.

Bond, G. L., & Bond, E. (1941). *Developmental reading in high school.* New York: Macmillan.

Brozo, W. G., & Simpson, M. L. (1999). *Readers, teachers, learners: Expanding literacy across the content areas* (3rd ed.). Upper Saddle River, NJ: Merrill.

Irvin, J. L. (1998). *Reading and the middle school student: Strategies to enhance literacy* (2nd ed.). Boston: Allyn & Bacon.

McCombs, B. L., & Barton, M. L. (1998). Motivating secondary school students to read their textbooks. *NASSP Bulletin, 82*(600), 24–33.

McKenna, M., Ellsworth, R. A., & Kear, D. (1995). Children's attitudes toward reading: A national survey. *Reading Research Quarterly, 30,* 934–957.

Weinstein, C. E., & Mayer, R. E. (1986). The teaching of learning strategies. In M. C. Wittrock (Ed.), *Handbook of research on teaching* (3rd ed., pp. 315–327). New York: Macmillan.

### Adolescents deserve assessment that shows them their strengths as well as their needs and that guides their teachers to design instruction that will best help them grow as readers.

Bauer, E. B. (1999). The promise of alternative literacy assessments in the classroom: A review of empirical studies. *Reading Research and Instruction, 38,* 153–168.

Darling-Hammond, L., Ancess, J., & Falk, B. (1995). *Authentic assessment in action: Studies of schools and students at work.* New York: Teachers College Press.

Hansen, J. (1998). *When learners evaluate.* Portsmouth, NH: Heinemann.

Mitchell, R., Willis, M., & The Chicago Teachers Union Quest Center. (1995). *Learning in overdrive: Designing curriculum, instruction, and assessment from standards.* Golden, CO: North America Press.

Olson, L. (1999). Making every test count: Testing raises a host of concerns. *Education Week, 18*(17), 11–20.

Pearson, P. D. (1998). Standards and assessments: Tools for crafting effective instruction? In J. L. F. Osborn (Ed.), *Learning to read* (pp. 264–288). New York: Guilford.

Stiggins, R. J. (1997). *Student-centered classroom assessment* (2nd ed.). Upper Saddle River, NJ: Merrill.

Tierney, R. J., & Clark, C. (with Fenner, L., Herter, R. J., Simpson, C. S., & Wiser, B.). (1998). Theory and research into practice: Portfolios: Assumptions, tensions, and possibilities. *Reading Research Quarterly, 33,* 474–486.

U.S. Department of Education. (1996). *Guidance on standards, assessment, and accountability.* Washington, DC: Author.

Wiggins, G. M., Jr. (1998). *Understanding by design.* Alexandria, VA: Association for Supervision and Curriculum Development.

**Adolescents deserve expert teachers who model and provide explicit instruction in reading comprehension and study strategies across the curriculum.**

Alvermann, D. E., & Phelps, S. F. (1998). *Content area reading and literacy: Succeeding in today's diverse classrooms* (2nd ed.). Boston: Allyn & Bacon.

Borko, H., & Putnam, R. T. (1996). Learning to teach. In D. C. Berliner, & R. C. Calfee (Eds.), *Handbook of educational psychology* (pp. 673–708). New York: Macmillan.

Gall, M. D., Gall, J. P., Jacobsen, D. R., & Bullock, T. L. (1990). *Tools for learning: A guide to teaching study skills*. Alexandria, VA: Association for Supervision and Curriculum Development.

Pearson, P. D., & Fielding, L. (1991). Comprehension instruction. In R. Barr, M. L. Kamil, P. B. Mosenthal, & P. D. Pearson (Eds.), *Handbook of reading research* (Vol. II, pp. 815–860). White Plains, NY: Longman.

Rosenshine, B., & Meister, C. (1992). The use of scaffolds for teaching higher-level cognitive strategies. *Educational Leadership, 50,* 26–33.

Symons, S., Richards, C., & Greene, C. (1995). Cognitive strategies for reading comprehension. In E. Wood, V. E. Woloshyn, & T. Willoughby (Eds.), *Cognitive strategy instruction for middle and high schools* (pp. 66–87). Cambridge, MA: Brookline.

Vacca, R. T., & Vacca, J. L. (1999). *Content area reading: Literacy and learning across the curriculum* (6th ed.). New York: Longman.

Weinstein, C. E., & Hume, L. M. (1998). *Study strategies for lifelong learning*. Washington, DC: American Psychological Association.

**Adolescents deserve reading specialists who assist individual students having difficulty learning how to read.**

Allen, J. (1995). *It's never too late: Leading adolescents to lifelong literacy*. Portsmouth, NH: Heinemann.

Anderson, V., & Roit, M. (1993). Planning and implementing collaborative strategy instruction for delayed readers in grades 6–10. *The Elementary School Journal, 94,* 121–138.

Barry, A. L. (1997). High school reading programs revisited. *Journal of Adolescent & Adult Literacy, 40,* 524–531.

Davidson, J., & Koppenhaver, D. (1993). *Adolescent literacy: What works and why* (2nd ed.). New York: Garland.

Kos, R. (1991). Persistence of reading difficulties: The voices of four middle school students. *American Educational Research Journal, 28,* 875–895.

Mehan, H., Hubbard, L., & Villanueva, I. (1996). *Constructing school success: The consequences of untracking low achieving students*. New York: Cambridge University Press.

Moore, D. W., Readence, J. E., & Rickelman, R. J. (1983). An historical exploration of content area reading instruction. *Reading Research Quarterly, 18,* 419–438.

O'Brien, D. (1998). Multiple literacies in a high-school program for "at-risk" adolescents. In D. E. Alvermann, K. A. Hinchman, D. W. Moore, S. E. Phelps, & D. R. Waff (Eds.), *Reconceptualizing the literacies in adolescents' lives* (pp. 27–49). Mahwah, NJ: Erlbaum.

Roller, C. M. (1996). *Variability not disability: Struggling readers in a workshop classroom*. Newark, DE: International Reading Association.

Rose, M. (1989). *Lives on the boundary: The struggles and achievements of America's underprepared*. New York: Free Press.

U.S. Department of Education, National Center for Education Statistics. (1997). *The condition of education, 1997* (NCES 97-388). Washington, DC: U.S. Government Printing Office.

*Adolescents deserve teachers who are trained to understand the complexities of individual adolescent readers, respect their differences, and respond to their characteristics.*

Beane, J. A. (1990). *A middle school curriculum: From rhetoric to reality*. Columbus, OH: National Middle School Association.

Diamond, B. J., & Moore, M. A. (1995). *Multicultural literacy: Mirroring the reality of the classroom*. White Plains, NY: Longman.

Dias, P. X. (1992). Literary reading and classroom constraints: Aligning practice with theory. In J. A. Langer (Ed.), *Literature instruction* (pp. 131–162). Urbana, IL: National Council of Teachers of English.

Finders, M. J. (1998/1999). Raging hormones: Stories of adolescence and implications for teacher preparation. *Journal of Adolescent & Adult Literacy, 42,* 252–263.

Hynds, S. (1997). *On the brink: Negotiating literature and life with adolescents.* New York: Teachers College Press.

Marzano, R. J. (1992). *A different kind of classroom.* Alexandria, VA: Association for Supervision and Curriculum Development.

National Middle School Association. (1992). *This we believe: Developmentally responsive middle level schools.* Columbus, OH: Author.

Rief, L. (1992). *Seeking diversity.* Portsmouth, NH: Heinemann.

*Adolescents deserve homes, communities, and a nation that will support their efforts to achieve advanced levels of literacy and provide the support necessary for them to succeed.*

Alvarez, M. (1998). Adolescent literacy: Are we in contact? In E. Sturtevant, E. J. Dugan, P. Linder, & W. Linek (Eds.), *Literacy and community* (20th yearbook of the College Reading Association, pp. 2–10). Commerce, TX: College Reading Association.

Anders, P. (1998). The literacy council: People are the key to an effective program. *NASSP Bulletin, 82*(600), 16–23.

Epstein, J. L. (1995). Creating school/family/community partnerships: Caring for the children we share. *Phi Delta Kappan, 76,* 701–712.

Graham, P. A. (1992). *SOS: Sustain our schools.* New York: Hill & Wang.

Humphries, J. W., Lipsitz, J., McGovern, J. T., & Wasser, J. D. (1997). Supporting the development of young adolescent readers. *Phi Delta Kappan, 79,* 305–311.

Moore, D. W. (1996). Contexts for literacy in secondary schools. In D. J. Leu, C. K. Kinzer, & K. A. Hinchman (Eds.), *Literacies for the 21st century: Research and practice* (45th yearbook of the National Reading Conference, pp. 15–46). Chicago: National Reading Conference.

National Association of Secondary School Principals. (1996). *Breaking ranks: Changing an American institution.* Reston, VA: Author.

Newmann, F. M. (1996). *Authentic achievement: Restructuring schools for intellectual quality.* San Francisco: Jossey-Bass.

# References

Allen, J. (2000). *Yellow brick roads: Shared and guided paths to independent reading 4–12.* York, ME: Stenhouse.

Allington, R. L. (2001). *What really matters for struggling readers: Designing research-based programs.* New York: Longman.

Allington, R. L. (2002a). What I've learned about effective reading instruction from a decade of studying exemplary elementary classrooms. *Phi Delta Kappan, 83,* 740–747.

Allington, R. L. (2002b, November). You can't learn much from books you can't read. *Educational Leadership, 60*(3), 16–19.

Allington, R. L. (2004, March). Setting the record straight. *Educational Leadership, 61*(6), 22–25.

Allington, R. L., & Johnston, P. H. (Eds.). (2002). *Reading to learn: Lessons from exemplary fourth-grade classrooms.* New York: Guilford Press.

Alvermann, D. E. (1991). The discussion web: A graphic aid for learning across the curriculum. *The Reading Teacher, 45,* 92–99.

Alvermann, D. E. (2002). Effective literacy instruction for adolescents. *Journal of Literacy Research, 34*(2), 189–208.

Alvermann, D. E., & Moore, D. W. (1991). Secondary school reading. In R. Barr, M. L. Kamil, P. Mosenthal, & P. D. Pearson (Eds.), *Handbook of reading research* (Vol. 2, pp. 951–983). New York: Longman.

Alvermann, D. E., & Rush, L. S. (2004). Literacy intervention programs at the middle and high school levels. In T. L. Jetton & J. A. Dole (Eds.), *Adolescent literacy research and practice* (pp. 210–227). New York: Guilford Press.

Amrein, A. L., & Berliner, D. C. (2002). *High-stakes testing, uncertainty, and student learning.* Educational Policy Analysis Archives, 10 (18). [Online]. Available: http://epaa.asu.edu/epaa/v10n18.

Anderson, R. C., & Biddle, W. B. (1975). On asking people questions about what they are reading. In G. H. Bower (Ed.), *The psychology of learning and motivation* (Vol. 9, pp. 9–129). New York: Academic Press.

Anderson, R. C., Wilson, P. T., & Fielding, L. G. (1988). Growth in reading and how children spend their time outside school. *Reading Research Quarterly, 23,* 285–303.

Applebee, A. (1996). *Curriculum as conversation: Transforming traditions of teaching and learning.* Chicago: University of Chicago Press.

Applebee, A., Langer, J., Nystrand, M., & Gamoran, A. (2003). Discussion-based approaches to developing understanding: Classroom instruction and student performance in middle and high school English. *American Educational Research Journal, 40,* 685–730.

Arnau, L., Kahrs, J., & Kruskamp, B. (2004). Peer coaching: Veteran high school teachers take the lead on learning. *NASSP Bulletin, 88,* 26–41.

Ashton-Warner, S. (1959). *Spinster.* New York: Simon & Schuster.

Avi. (1988). *Romeo and Juliet together (and alive!) at last.* New York: HarperTrophy.

Baumann, J. F., Kame'enui, E. J., & Ash, G. E. (2003). Research on vocabulary instruction: Voltaire redux. In J. Flood, D. Lapp, J. R. Squire, & J. M. Jensen (Eds.), *Handbook of research on teaching the English language arts* (2nd ed., pp. 752–785). Mahwah, NJ: Lawrence Erlbaum Associates.

Bean, R. (2003). *The reading specialist: Leadership for the classroom, school, and community.* New York: Guilford Press.

Bean, R., Cassidy, J., Grumet, J., Shelton, D., & Wallis, S. (2002). What do reading specialists do? Results from a national survey. *The Reading Teacher, 55,* 736–744.

Bean, R., Swan, A., & Knaub, R. (2003). Reading specialists in schools with exemplary programs: Functional, versatile, and prepared. *The Reading Teacher, 56,* 446–454.

Bear, D. R., Invernizzi, M., Templeton, S., & Johnston, F. (2003). *Words their way* (3rd ed.). Upper Saddle River, NJ: Merrill/Prentice Hall.

Betts, E. A. (1946). *Foundations of reading instruction.* New York: American Books.

Blachowicz, C., & Fisher, P. J. (2002). *Teaching vocabulary in all classrooms* (2nd ed.). Upper Saddle River, NJ: Merrill/Prentice Hall.

Bomer, R. (1999). Conferring with struggling readers: The test of our craft, courage, and hope. *The New Advocate, 12,* 21–38.

Brassell, D., & Flood, J. (2004). *Vocabulary strategies every teacher needs to know.* San Diego, CA: Academic Professional Development.

Bridges, R. (1999). *Through my eyes.* New York: Scholastic.

Broaddus, K., & Bloodgood, J. (1999). "We're already supposed to know how to teach reading": Teacher change to support struggling readers. *Reading Research Quarterly, 34,* 426–451.

Brown, R. G. (1991). *Schools of thought: How the politics of literacy shape thinking in the classroom.* San Francisco: Jossey-Bass.

Browne, A. (1998). *Voices in the park.* New York: Dorling Kindersley.

Brozo, W. G. (2002, December). *Tales out of school: Accounting for adolescents in a literacy reform community.* Paper presented at the meeting of the National Reading Conference, Miami, FL.

Brozo, W. G., & Hargis, C. H. (2003). Taking seriously the idea of reform: One high school's efforts to make reading more responsive to all students. *Journal of Adolescent & Adult Literacy, 47,* 14–23.

Calabro, M. (1999). *The perilous journey of the Donner party.* New York: Clarion.

Calhoun, E. (2004). *Using data to assess your reading program.* Alexandria, VA: Association for Supervision and Curriculum Development.

Calkins, L. M. (2001). *The art of teaching reading.* New York: Teachers College.

Campbell, J., Donahue, P., Reese, C., & Phillips, G. (1996). *National Assessment of Educational Progress 1994 reading report card for the nation and the states.* Washington, DC: National Center for Education Statistics, U.S. Department of Education.

Carter, C. J. (1997). Why reciprocal teaching? *Educational Leadership. 54*(6), 64–69.

Clay, M. M. (2001). *Change over time in children's literacy development.* Portsmouth, NH: Heinemann.

Collicutt, P. (2002). *This car.* New York: Farrar, Straus, and Giroux.

Crowe, C. (2003). *Getting away with murder: The true story of the Emmett Till case.* New York: Dial.

Dahl, R. (1966). *The magic finger.* New York: Scholastic.

Daniels, H. (2002). *Literature circles: Voice and choice in book clubs and reading groups* (2nd ed.). York, ME: Stenhouse.

Darling-Hammond, L., & Falk, B. (1997). Using standards and assessments to support student learning. *Phi Delta Kappan, 79,* 190–199.

Dixon, C., & Nessel, D. (1983). *Language experience approach to reading (and writing): Language-experience reading for second language learners.* Hayward, CA: Alemany.

Draper, S. M. (2001). *Romiette and Julio.* New York: Simon Pulse.

Duke, N. K., & Pearson, P. D. (2002). Effective practices for developing reading comprehension. In A. Farstrup & J. Samuels (Eds.), *What research has to say about reading instruction* (3rd ed., pp. 205–242). Newark, DE: International Reading Association.

Dwyer, E. J., & Reed, V. (1989). Effects of sustained silent reading on attitudes toward reading. *Reading Horizons, 29,* 283–293.

Faber, J. E., Morris, J. D., & Lieberman, M. G. (2000). The effect of note taking on ninth grade students' comprehension. *Reading Psychology, 21,* 257–270.

Farnan, N., Flood, J., & Lapp, D. (1994). Comprehending through reading and writing: Six research-based instructional strategies. In K. Spangenberg-Urbschat & R. Pritchard (Eds.), *Kids come in all languages: Reading instruction for ESL students* (pp. 135–157). Newark, DE: International Reading Association.

Fearn, L., & Farnan, N. (2001). *Interactions: Teaching writing and the language arts.* Boston: Houghton Mifflin.

Fehring, H., & Green, P. (Eds.). (2001). *Critical literacy: A collection of articles from the Australian literacy educator's association.* Melbourne, Australia: Intrados Group.

Fisher, D. (2001a). Trust the process: Increasing student achievement via professional development and process accountability. *NASSP Bulletin: The Journal for Middle Level and High School Leaders, 85*(629), 67–71.

Fisher, D. (2001b). "We're moving on up": Creating a schoolwide literacy effort in an urban high school. *Journal of Adolescent & Adult Literacy, 45,* 92–101.

Fisher, D. (2004). Setting the "opportunity to read" standard: Resuscitating the SSR program in an urban high school. *Journal of Adolescent & Adult Literacy, 48,* 138–151.

Fisher, D., Flood, J., Lapp, D., & Frey, N. (2004). Interactive read-alouds: Is there a common set of implementation practices? *The Reading Teacher, 58*(1), 8–17.

Fisher, D., & Frey, N. (2003). Writing instruction for struggling adolescent readers: A gradual release model. *Journal of Adolescent & Adult Literacy, 46*(5), 396–407.

Fisher, D., & Frey, N. (2004). *Improving adolescent literacy: Strategies at work.* Upper Saddle River, NJ: Merrill/Prentice Hall.

Fisher, D., Frey, N., Farnan, N., Fearn, L., & Petersen, F. (2004). Increasing writing achievement in an urban middle school. *Middle School Journal, 36*(2), 21–26

Fisher, D., Frey, N., & Williams, D. (2002, November). Seven literacy strategies that work. *Educational Leadership, 60*(3), 70–73.

Fisher, D., Lapp, D., & Flood, J. (2005). Consensus scoring and peer planning: Meeting accountability demands one school at a time. *The Reading Teacher, 58,* 656–666.

Fisher, D., Sax, C., & Pumpian, I. (1999). *Inclusive high schools: Learning from contemporary classrooms.* Baltimore: Paul H. Brookes.

Fleischman, P. (1993). *Bull Run.* New York: HarperTrophy.

Fleischman, P. (1997). *Seedfolks.* New York: Scholastic.

Flood, J., Lapp, D., Squire, J. R., & Jensen, J. M. (2003). *Handbook of research on teaching the English language arts* (2nd ed.). Mahwah, NJ: Lawrence Erlbaum Associates.

Fox, P. (1993). *Monkey island.* New York: Dell.

Frey, N., & Fisher, D. (2007). *Language arts workshop: Purposeful reading and writing instruction.* Upper Saddle River, NJ: Merrill/Prentice Hall.

Gallaz, C., & Innocenti, R. (1985). *Rose Blanche*. Mankato, MN: Creative Education.

Ganske, L. (1981). Note taking: A significant and integral part of learning environments. *Educational Communication and Technology: A Journal of Theory, Research, and Development, 29,* 155–175.

Gardner, R. (2004). *Light, sound, and waves science fair projects: Using sunglasses, guitars, CDs, and other stuff.* Berkeley Heights, NJ: Enslow Publishers.

Gee, J. P. (1996). *Social linguistics and literacies: Ideology in discourses* (2nd ed.). London: Falmer.

Glass, A. (2001). *Mountain men: True grit and tall tales.* New York: Doubleday.

Goodman, Y., & Marek, A. (1996). *Retrospective miscue analysis: Revaluing readers and reading.* Katonah, NY: R. C. Owens Publishers.

Gottesman, B. (2000). *Peer coaching for educators* (2nd ed.). Lanham, MD: Scarecrow Education.

Greenleaf, C., Schoenbach, R., Cziko, C., & Mueller, F. (2001). Apprenticing adolescent readers to academic literacy. *Harvard Educational Review, 71,* 79–129.

Guiney, E. (2001). Coaching isn't just for athletes: The role of teacher leaders. *Phi Delta Kappan, 82*(10), 740–743.

Guthrie, J. T. (2002). Preparing students for high-stakes test taking in reading. In A. E. Farstrup & S. J. Samuels (Eds.), *What research has to say about reading instruction* (pp. 370–391). Newark, DE: International Reading Association.

Hakim, J. (2002). *Liberty for all?* (*A history of us*) (3rd ed.). New York: Oxford University Press.

Hampton, W. (2001). *Meltdown: A race against nuclear disaster at Three Mile Island.* Cambridge, MA: Candlewick Press.

Hansen, J. (1981). The effects of inference training and practice on young children's reading comprehension. *Reading Research Quarterly, 16*(3), 391–417.

Harklau, L. (2001). From high school to college: Student perspectives on literacy practices. *Journal of Literacy Research, 33,* 32–70.

Head, M. H., & Readence, J. E. (1986). Anticipation guides: Meaning through prediction. In E. K. Dishner, T. W. Bean, J. E. Readence, & D. W. Moore (Eds.), *Reading in the content areas: Improving classroom instruction* (2nd ed., pp. 229–234). Dubuque, IA: Kendall/Hunt.

Herll, S., & O'Drobinak, B. (2004). Role of the coach: Dream keeper, supporter, friend. *Journal of Staff Development, 25*(2), 42–45.

Hiebert, E. (1991). *Literacy for a diverse society: Perspectives, policies, and practices.* New York: Teachers College Press.

Hoy, W. K., Tarter, C. J., & Kottkamp, R. B. (1991). *Open schools/healthy schools.* Newbury Park, CA: Sage.

Hull, G. A., & Rose, M. (1989). Rethinking remediation: Toward a social-cognitive understanding of problematic reading and writing. *Written Communication, 8,* 139–154.

Hynd, C. R. (1999). Teaching students to think critically using multiple texts in history. *Journal of Adolescent & Adult Literacy, 42,* 428–436.

International Reading Association. (2000). *Teaching all children to read: The role of the reading specialist.* Newark, DE: International Reading Association.

International Reading Association. (2006). *Standards for middle and high school literacy coaches.* New York: Carnegie Corporation.

Ivey, G. (2002, November). Getting started: Manageable literacy practices. *Educational Leadership, 60*(3), 20–23.

Ivey, G. (2003). "The teacher makes it more explainable" and other reasons to read aloud in the intermediate grades. *The Reading Teacher, 56,* 812–814.

Ivey, G. (2004). Content counts with urban struggling readers. In D. Lapp, C. C. Block, E. J. Cooper, J. Flood, N. Roser, & J. V. Tinajero (Eds.). *Teaching all the children: Strategies for developing literacy in an urban setting* (pp. 316–326). New York: Guilford Press.

Ivey, G., & Baker, M. (2004). Phonics instruction for older students? Just say no. *Educational Leadership, 61*(6), 35–39.

Ivey, G., & Broaddus, K. (2001). "Just plain reading": A survey of what makes students want to read in middle school classrooms. *Reading Research Quarterly, 36,* 350–377.

Ivey, G., & Broaddus, K. (2003, December). *"It's good to read if you can read it": What matters to middle school students in content area independent reading.* Paper presented at the National Reading Conference, Scottsdale, AZ.

Ivey, G., & Broaddus, K. (2004). *Figuring out literacy engagement for adolescent Latina/o students just beginning to read and write in English.* Paper presented at the National Reading Conference, San Antonio, TX.

Jago, C. (2002). *Cohesive writing: Why concept is not enough.* Portsmouth, NH: Heinemann.

Jiménez, F. (1997). *The circuit.* Albuquerque, NM: University of New Mexico Press.

Johnston, P. (2003). Assessment conversations. *The Reading Teacher, 57,* 90–92.

Johnston, P. H. (1987). Teachers as evaluation experts. *The Reading Teacher, 40,* 744–748.

Johnston, P. H., & Allington, R. L. (1991). Remediation. In R. Barr, M. L. Kamil, P. Mosenthal, & P. D. Pearson (Eds.), *Handbook of reading research* (Vol. 2, pp. 984–1012). New York: Longman.

Johnston, P. H., & Winograd, P. (1985). Passive failure in reading. *Journal of Reading Behavior, 17,* 279–299.

Jorgensen, C. M. (December 1994–January 1995). Essential questions—Inclusive answers. *Educational Leadership, 52*(4), 52–55.

Joyce, B., & Showers, B. (2002). *Student achievement through staff development* (3rd ed.). Alexandria, VA: Association for Supervision and Curriculum Development.

Kasper-Ferguson, S., & Moxley, R. A. (2002, May). Developing a writing package with student graphing of fluency. *Education and Treatment of Children, 25*(2), 249–267.

Keene, E. O., & Zimmerman, S. (1997). *Mosaic of thought: Teaching comprehension in a reader's workshop.* Portsmouth, NH: Heinemann.

Kennedy, C. H., & Fisher, D. (2001). *Inclusive middle schools.* Baltimore: Paul H. Brookes.

King, C., & Osborne, L. B. (1997). *Oh freedom! Kids talk about the civil rights movement with the people who made it happen.* New York: Knopf.

King, M. L., Jr. (1997). *I have a dream.* New York: Scholastic.

Knapp, M. S., & Turnbull, B. (1991). *Better schools for the children in poverty: Alternatives to conventional wisdom.* Berkeley, CA: McCutchan.

Krashen, S. (1993). *The power of reading: Insights from the research.* Englewood, CO: Libraries Unlimited.

Krashen, S. (2001, October). More smoke and mirrors: A critique of the National Reading Panel report on fluency. *Phi Delta Kappan, 83,* 119–123.

Krashen, S. (2004). False claims about literacy development. *Educational Leadership, 61,* 18–21.

Kucer, S. (2005). *Dimensions of literacy: A conceptual base for teaching reading and writing in school settings* (2nd ed.). Mahwah, NJ, Lawrence Erlbaum.

Kuhn, M. R., & Stahl, S. A. (2000). *Fluency: A review of developmental and remedial practices* (Report No. 2-008). Ann Arbor, MI: Center for the Improvement of Early Reading Achievement.

Lam, S., Yim, P., & Lam, T. W. (2002). Transforming school culture: Can true collaboration be initiated? *Educational Research, 44,* 181–195.

Langer, G. M., Colton, A. B., & Goff, L. S. (2003). *Collaborative analysis of student work: Improving teaching and learning.* Alexandria, VA: Association for Supervision and Curriculum Development.

Langer, J. (2000). *Teaching middle and high school students to read and write well: Six features of effective instruction.* Albany, NY: National Research Center on English Learning and Achievement.

Langer, J. (2002). *Effective literacy instruction: Building successful reading and writing programs.* Urbana, IL: National Council of Teachers of English.

Langer, J. A. (2001). Beating the odds: Teaching middle and high school students to read and write well. *American Educational Research Journal, 38,* 837–880.

Lapp, D., Fisher, D., Flood, J., & Cabello, A. (2001). An integrated approach to the teaching and assessment of language arts. In S. R. Hurley & J. V. Tinajero (Eds.), *Literacy assessment of second language learners* (pp. 1–26). Needham Heights, MA: Allyn & Bacon.

Lapp, D., Fisher, D., Flood, J., & Frey, N. (2003). Dual role of the urban reading specialist. *Journal of Staff Development, 24* (2), 33–37

Leslie, L., & Caldwell, J. (2005). *Qualitative reading inventory-4* (4th ed.). Boston: Allyn & Bacon.

Luke, A. (1995–1996). Text and discourse in education: An introduction to critical discourse analysis. In M. W. Apple (Ed.), *Review of Research in Education* (Vol. 21, pp. 3–48). Washington, DC: American Educational Research Association.

Madaus, G. (1998). The distortion of teaching and testing: High-stakes testing and instruction, *Peabody Journal of Education, 65,* 29–46.

Mallette, M. H., Henk, W. A., & Melnick, S. A. (2004). The influence of Accelerated Reader on the affective literacy orientations of intermediate grade students. *Journal of Literacy Research, 36,* 73–84.

Marzano, R. J. (2004). *Building background knowledge for academic achievement: Research on what works in schools.* Alexandria, VA: Association for Supervision and Curriculum Development.

McCarrier, A., Pinnell, G. S., & Fountas, I. C. (2000). *Interactive writing: How language and literacy come together, K–2.* Portsmouth, NH: Heinemann.

McClafferty, C. K. (2001). *The head bone's connected to the neck bone: The weird, wacky, and wonderful x-ray.* New York: Farrar, Straus, and Giroux.

Mercati, C. (2000). *Kit Carson: A life of adventure.* Logan, IA: Perfection Learning.

Moje, E. B. (2002). Re-framing adolescent literacy research for new times: Studying youth as a resource. *Reading Research and Instruction, 41,* 211–228.

Moje, E. B., Young, J. P., Readence, J. E., & Moore, D. W. (2000). Reinventing adolescent literacy for new times: Perennial millennial issues. *Journal of Adolescent & Adult Literacy, 43,* 400–410.

Montgomery, S. (2001). *The man-eating tigers of Sundarbans.* Boston: Houghton Mifflin.

Mooney, J., & Cole, D. (2000). *Learning outside the lines: Two Ivy League students with learning disabilities and ADHD give you the tools for academic success and educational revolution.* New York: Fireside.

Moore, D., Bean, T., Birdyshaw, D., & Rycik, J. (1999). *Adolescent literacy: A position statement.* Newark, DE: International Reading Association.

Morgan, W. (1997). *Critical literacy in the classroom: The art of the possible.* New York: Routledge.

Morrison, T. (2004). *Remember: The journey to school integration.* Boston: Houghton Mifflin.

Moss, B., & Hendershot, J. (2002). Exploring sixth graders' selection of nonfiction trade books. *The Reading Teacher, 56,* 6–17.

Myers, W. D. (1991). *Now is your time! The African-American struggle for freedom.* New York: HarperTrophy.

Myers, W. D. (2004). *I've seen the promised land: The life of Dr. Martin Luther King, Jr.* New York: HarperCollins.

Nagy, W. E., & Anderson, R. C. (1984). How many words are there in printed school English? *Reading Research Quarterly, 19,* 304–330.

National Reading Panel. (2000). *Teaching children to read: An evidence-based assessment of the scientific research literature on reading and its implications for reading instruction.* Washington, DC: National Institute of Child Health and Human Development.

Neuman, S. B. (1999). Books make a difference: A study of access to literacy. *Reading Research Quarterly, 34,* 286–311.

Newmann, F., King, B., & Rigdon, M. (1997). Accountability and school performance: Implications from restructuring schools. *Harvard Educational Review, 67,* 41–74.

Oczkus, L. D. (2003). *Reciprocal teaching at work: Strategies for improving reading comprehension.* Newark, DE: International Reading Association.

Ogle, D. M. (1986). K-W-L: A teaching model that develops active reading of expository text. *The Reading Teacher, 39,* 564–570.

Optiz, M. F., & Rasinski, T. V. (1998). *Good-bye round robin: 25 effective oral reading strategies.* Portsmouth, NH: Heinemann.

Palincsar, A. S., & Brown, A. (1984). Reciprocal teaching of comprehension-fostering and comprehension monitoring activities. *Cognition and Instruction, 1*(2), 117–175.

Parks, R. (1997). *I am Rosa Parks.* New York: Puffin.

Pauk, W. (2001). *How to study in college* (7th ed.). Boston: Houghton Mifflin College.

Pearson, P. D., & Fielding, L. (1991). Comprehension instruction. In R. Barr, M. L. Kamil, P. Mosenthal, & P. D. Pearson (Eds.), *Handbook of reading research* (Vol. II, pp. 815–860). Mahwah, NJ: Erlbaum.

Peverly, S. T., Brobst, K. E., Graham, M., & Shaw, R. (2003). College adults are not good at self-regulation: A study on the relationship of self-regulation, note taking, and test taking. *Journal of Educational Psychology, 95,* 335–346.

Pilgreen, J. J. (2001). *The SSR handbook: How to organize and manage a sustained silent reading program.* Portsmouth, NH: Boynton/Cook Publishers.

Pryor, B. (1999). *Joseph: 1861—Rumble of war.* New York: Morrow.

Rappaport, D. (2001). *Martin's big words: The life of Dr. Martin Luther King, Jr.* New York: Hyperion Books for Children.

Reeder, C. (1997). *Across the lines.* New York: Avon.

Ringgold, F. (1995). *My dream of Martin Luther King.* New York: Dragonfly.

Robinson, D. H. (1998). Graphic organizers as aids to text learning. *Reading Research and Instruction, 37,* 85–105.

Santa, C., & Havens, L. (1995). *Creating independence through student-owned strategies: Project CRISS.* Dubuque, IA: Kendall/Hunt.

Shulman, I. (1961). *West side story.* New York: Pocket.

Simon, S. (2002). *Planets around the sun.* New York: Seastar Books.

Singer, M. (2001). *Tough beginnings: How baby animals survive.* New York: Holt.

Sizer, T. (1992). *Horace's compromise: The dilemma of the American high school.* Boston: Houghton Mifflin.

Slater, W. H. (2004). Teaching English from a literacy perspective: The goal of high literacy for all students. In T. L. Jetton & J. A. Dole (Eds.), *Adolescent literacy research and practice* (pp. 40–58). New York: Guilford.

Smith, M. I. (1991). Put to the test: The effects of external testing on teachers. *Educational Researcher, 20*(5), 8–11.

Spires, H. A., & Stone, P. D. (1989). The directed note-taking activity: A self-questioning approach. *Journal of Reading, 33,* 36–39.

Squire, J. R. (Ed.). (1987). *The dynamics of learning language: Research in reading and English.* Urbana, IL: ERIC Clearinghouse on Reading and Communication Skills.

Stahl, S. (1998). *Vocabulary development.* Newton Upper Falls, MA: Brookline.

Stanovich, K. (1986). Matthew effects in reading: Some consequences of individual differences in the acquisition of literacy. *Reading Research Quarterly, 21,* 360–406.

Steffy, B. E., & Wolfe, M. P. (2001). A life-cycle model for career teachers. *Kappa Delta Pi Record, 38*(1), 16–19.

Steffy, B. E., Wolfe, M. P., Pasch, S. H., & Enz, B. J. (Eds.). (2000). *Life cycle of the career teacher.* Thousand Oaks, CA: Corwin Press.

Stewart, R. A., Paradis, E. E., Ross, B., & Lewis, M. J. (1996). Student voices: What works best in literature-based developmental reading. *Journal of Adolescent & Adult Literacy, 39,* 468–478.

Street, B. (1995). *Social literacies: Critical approaches to literacy in development, ethnography, and education.* London: Longman.

Swados, E. (2002). *Hey you! C'mere: A poetry slam.* New York: Arthur A. Levine.

Szymusiak, K., & Sibberson, F. (2001). *Beyond leveled books: Supporting transitional readers in grades 2–5.* York, ME: Stenhouse.

Tanaka, S. (2003). *A day that changed America: Gettysburg.* New York: Hyperion.

Taylor, B. M., Anderson, R. C., Au, K. H., & Raphael, T. E. (1999). *Discretion in the translation of reading research to policy* (Report No. 3-006). Ann Arbor, MI: Center for the Improvement of Early Reading Achievement.

Taylor, B. M., Pearson, P. D., Clark, K., & Walpole, S. (2000). Effective schools and accomplished teachers: Lessons about primary-grade reading instruction in low-income schools. *Elementary School Journal, 101,* 121–165.

Tinajero, J. V., & Ada, A. F. (Eds.). (1993). *The power of two languages: Literacy and biliteracy for Spanish-speaking students.* New York: Macmillan/McGraw-Hill.

Tsuchiya, Y. (1988). *Faithful elephants: A true story of animals, people, and war.* Boston: Houghton Mifflin.

Vacca, R. T., & Vacca, J. L. (2001). *Content area reading: Literacy and learning across the curriculum* (7th ed.). Boston: Pearson Allyn & Bacon.

Valencia, S. W., & Buly, M. R. (2004). Behind test scores: What struggling readers really need. *The Reading Teacher, 57,* 520–531.

Vaughn, S., Moody, S. W., & Schumm, J. S. (1998). Broken promises: Reading instruction in the resource room. *Exceptional Children, 64,* 211–225.

Villa, R. A., Thousand, J. S., & Nevin, A. I. (2004). *A guide to co-teaching: Practical tips for facilitating student learning.* Thousand Oaks, CA: Corwin Press.

Vonnegut, K. (1998). *Cat's cradle.* New York: Delta Trade Paperbacks.

Wiggins, G., & McTighe, J. (1998). *Understanding by design.* Alexandria, VA: Association for Supervision and Curriculum Development.

Wilhelm, J. D. (2001). *Improving comprehension with think-aloud strategies: Modeling what good readers do.* New York: Scholastic.

Winter, J. (1998). *My name is Georgia.* San Diego, CA: Harcourt Brace.

Wolf, D., & King, J. (Producers), & Van Sant, G. (Director). (2000). *Finding Forrester* [Motion picture]. United States: Columbia Pictures.

Wong, H. K. (2004). Induction programs that keep new teachers teaching and improving. *NASSP Bulletin, 88,* 41–58.

Wood, K. D., Lapp, D., & Flood, J. (1992). *Guiding readers through texts: A review of study guides.* Newark, DE: International Reading Association.

Worthy, J., Broaddus, K., & Ivey, G. (2001). *Pathways to independence: Reading, writing, and learning in grades 3–8.* New York: Guilford.

Worthy, J., & McKool, S. (1996). Students who say they hate to read: The importance of opportunity, choice, and access. In D. J. Leu, C. K. Kinzer, & K. A. Hinchman (Eds.), *Literacies for the 21st century: Research and practice. 45th yearbook of the National Reading Conference* (pp. 245–256). Chicago: National Reading Conference.

Worthy, J., Moorman, M., & Turner, M. (1999). What Johnny likes to read is hard to find in school. *Reading Research Quarterly, 34,* 12–27.

Worthy, J., Turner, M., & Moorman, M. (1998). The precarious place of self-selected reading. *Language Arts, 75,* 296–304.

# Index

Page references for figures are indicated with an *f* after the page numbers.

# About the Authors

**Gay Ivey** is an associate professor of reading education at James Madison University in Harrisonburg, Virginia. She is a former middle school reading/language arts teacher. Ivey's research and teaching expertise include examining ways to make regular classroom instruction more responsive to individual development and motivation, particularly for older students still learning to read and write. She can be reached at iveymg@jmu.edu.

**Douglas Fisher** is a professor of literacy and language education in the Department of Teacher Education at San Diego State University and the Director of Professional Development for the City Heights Educational Collaborative. He is the recipient of an International Reading Association Celebrate Literacy Award as well as a Christa McAuliffe award for excellence in teacher education. Fisher has published numerous articles on reading and literacy, differentiated instruction, and curriculum design as well as books, including *Improving Adolescent Literacy: Strategies at Work* and *Responsive Curriculum Design in Secondary Schools: Meeting the Diverse Needs of Students*. He has taught a variety of courses in SDSU's teacher-credentialing program as well as graduate-level courses on English language development and literacy. Fisher has also taught classes in English, writing, and literacy development to secondary school students. He can be reached at dfisher@mail.sdsu.edu.

**Related ASCD Resources**
**Literacy and Adolescents**

At the time of publication, the following resources were available; for the most up-to-date information about ASCD resources, go to www.ascd.org. ASCD stock numbers are noted in parentheses.

**Audio**
*Improving Reading Is Everyone's Business* by Brenda Hunter (Audiotape #203122S25; CD #503215S25)

*Literacy Matters Across the Curriculum* by Robin Fogarty and Brian Pete (Audiotape #204280S25; CD #504414S25)

**Mixed Media**
*The Multiple Intelligences of Reading and Writing: Making the Words Come Alive Books-in-Action Package* (10 Books and 1 Video) by Thomas Armstrong (#703381S25)

*Using Data to Assess Your Reading Program* (Book and CD-ROM) by Emily Calhoun (#102268S25)

**Networks**
Visit the ASCD Web site (www.ascd.org) and click on About ASCD. Go to the section on Networks for information about professional educators who have formed groups around topics such as "Language, Literacy, and Language" and "Middle Grades." Look in the Network Directory for current facilitators' addresses and phone numbers.

**Online Courses**
Visit the ASCD Web site (www.ascd.org) for the following professional development opportunities:

Helping Struggling Readers by Kathy Checkley (#PD04OC42)

Successful Strategies for Literacy and Learning by Angelika Machi (#PD03OC27)

**Print Products**
*Building Student Literacy Through Sustained Silent Reading* by Steve Gardiner (#105027S25)

*Educational Leadership, March 2004:* What Research Says About Reading (Entire Issue #104028S25)

*Educational Leadership, April 2005:* The Adolescent Learner (Entire Issue #105034S25)

*Educational Leadership, October 2005:* Reading Comprehension (Entire Issue #106037S25)

*Literacy Leadership For Grades 5–12* by Rosemarye Taylor and Valerie Doyle Collins (#103022S25)

*Literacy Strategies For Grades 4–12: Reinforcing The Threads Of Reading* by Karen Tankersley (#104428S25)

**Video**
*Implementing A Reading Program In Secondary Schools Video* (One 30-Minute Videotape With A Facilitator's Guide. #402033S25)

*The Lesson Collection: Literacy Strategies Tapes 49–56* (Eight 10- To 20-Minute Videotapes # 405160S25)

For more information, visit us on the World Wide Web (http://www.ascd.org), send an e-mail message to member@ascd.org, call the ASCD Service Center (1-800-933-ASCD or 703-578-9600, then press 2), send a fax to 703-575-5400, or write to Information Services, ASCD, 1703 N. Beauregard St., Alexandria, VA 22311-1714 USA.